Shoes of Glass, 2

BY LIBBY YALOM
The Shoe Lady

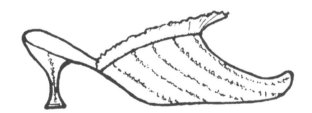

The Glass Press, Inc.
dba Antique Publications
P. O. Box 553 • Marietta, Ohio 45750

PB ISBN 1-57080-034-0
HB ISBN 1-57080-035-9

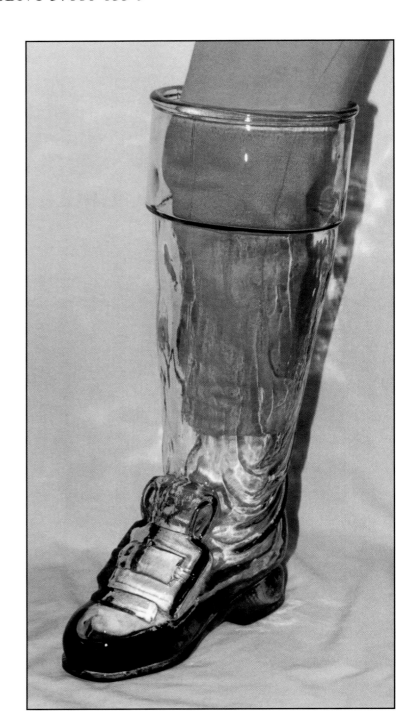

This book is dedicated to Cinderella
and Prince Charming, who started it all.
Also, to all the wonderful shoe collectors I have
come to know since I acquired my first shoe in 1971.

ACKNOWLEDGMENTS

My thanks to Joann Elmore whose help was indispensable during the three days of photographing for the first *Shoes of Glass* book. I also wish to thank the following people with Book One:

Frank Fenton for his help and advice with Fenton shoes and colors;

Erna Burris, Curator of the Degenhart Paperweight and Glass Museum, Inc., for her help with the Degenhart shoes and prices;

Tom Bredehoft for his help with identification of the Duncan shoes;

Norma Jenkins of the Rakow Library, Corning Museum of Glass;

Gwen Shumpert who first encouraged me to write about glass shoes;

and Tom Klopp for his help.

For their help with Book Two, my thanks to Joann Elmore, Neila and Tom Bredehoft, and Maggie Williamson. I wish to express my gratitude to the following people for their generosity in allowing shoes from their collections to be photographed for *Shoes of Glass 2*:

Shirley Barnett, Kansas; Pat Beguhl, Minnesota; Sharon Borgini, Illinois; Betty Brillhart, Missouri; Jennifer Chouinard, Maine; Erma Clements, Texas; Bill Crowl, West Virginia; Denis Doll, Minnesota; Joann Elmore, Maryland; Judy Foles, Virginia; Ruth Hammond, Kansas; June Hill, Florida; Cathy Kaufman, New York; Andrea Koppel, New York; Chloe McKinney, Washington; Jim Phillips, Maryland; Ann Quirk, Kansas; Bea Redfern, Pennsylvania; Tim Russell, Michigan; Mary Tanner, Texas; Rittie Ward, Texas; Maggie Williamson, Oklahoma; Anne Wojtkowski, Massachusetts; and Kathy Wujcik, Ohio.

Thanks to Jeremy Cantor and Mike Trovato for providing the wonderfully executed line drawings shown throughout Book One.

A very special thank you to Tarez Graban who made things go more smoothly than they would have otherwise.

Finally, thanks to my husband, Abe Yalom, who photographed all the additional shoes for Book One, as well as all the shoes for Book Two and the covers.

CONTENTS

INTRODUCTION 6

BOOK I 8

    COLOR PLATES 9

    CAPTIONS 97

BOOK II 154

    CAPTIONS 155

    COLOR PLATES 169

INDEX 201

BIBLIOGRAPHY 205

1998 VALUE GUIDE 207

INTRODUCTION

Author's note:

You will find this book contains much more than a reprinted edition of the first *Shoes of Glass*. It is separated into two sections, conveniently called Book One and Book Two. Book One contains a revised, updated edition of the first *Shoes of Glass*, featuring additional photography of similar shoes that have been collected over the last ten years in interesting patterns or colors. This book retains the same plate numbers (with the exception of plates 49 through 54 which I have purposely omitted) and shoe numbers (which have since become a shoe collector's standard).

I chose to omit plates 49 through 54 because I have not kept up with the shoes featured in those plates. This will account for the break in shoe numbers which occurs on pages 59 and 94.

Book Two consists of more of the new finds which have excited me over the years and for which I have been able to gather limited information. In some cases, these new shoes will be variations on similar moulds in Book One, representing rare or unusual colors, decorations or styles. However, in most cases they are completely new items which have been collected since the first *Shoes of Glass* was published.

If anyone has corrections or additions, such as makers, dates of manufacture, shoes not shown and colors not mentioned, I would be pleased to hear from you.

Libby Yalom
The Shoe Lady
P. O. Box 7146
Adelphi, MD 20783

When I first started collecting in 1971 I bought anything that looked like a shoe, and I have been told by other collectors that most of them started that way also. After a time, one gets much more selective. The most important thing is to buy what pleases you and what you can afford. I have never purchased any shoe for my collection with the thought of what it might be worth if and when I am ready to sell it.

PURCHASING SHOES

Collectors often ask me about buying a damaged shoe. If I find a shoe which I don't have or have never seen, and which has some damage, I will buy it if the price reflects the condition, just to have as an example. It may be many years before another is found and, if and when it is, one can upgrade then.

On occasion one sees a "pair" of shoes for sale, which in reality are simply two of the same shoe. However, some shoes are shaped on the sole as either right or left foot, and others come with buttons on the right or left side. Either of these examples, when put together, will make a true pair of shoes, but most shoes are straight in shape and are not considered a pair even though there may be two of them. Of course, if a collector wishes to collect duplicate shoe "pairs" he or she should do so. As I stated previously, a collector should collect what he or she finds pleasing.

Some shoes are sought after by collectors in other fields also, and that fact tends to raise the price on those particular items. The shoe night lamp by

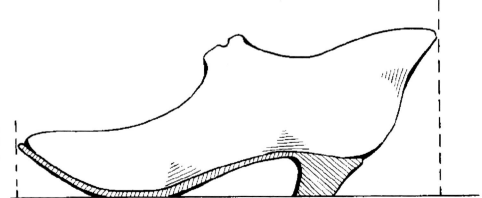

Figure A.
Measuring shoes
from back edge to toe edge.

Atterbury is a good example. It can seldom be found for less than $900.00 and I have seen it for much more. Also, the shoe thimble holders are prized by sewing collectors. Some of the other items are perfumes, inkwells, salts, candy containers and bottles.

CLEANING SHOES

The best way to clean a glass shoe, and some need cleaning badly, is to place it on a towel in the sink and spray it with an all-purpose cleaner such as 409. Let it sit for a minute and then rinse with warm water. A soft brush might be needed for some hard-to-reach areas. If there is decoration on the shoe, then a strong cleaner should not be used. A mild liquid detergent and warm water would suffice.

MEASURING SHOES

So that everyone will understand how I arrived at the dimensions given for all the shoes, please see Figure A. The longest and highest dimensions are always used. These can vary on the same style by $1/8$ to $3/16$ of an inch.

I often refer to Ruth Webb Lee, the author of *Victorian Glass*. In that book, her chapter on glass shoes has been the only extensive reference material on the subject since it was written in the 1940s.

CATALOGUING SHOES

There are many places where shoes may be found and none of these should be overlooked. In addition to antique shows and flea markets there are estate sales, yard sales, auctions, antique shops, antique malls, gift shops and department stores. Don't overlook the catalogs which come in the mail. Number 423 was purchased that way in 1986 (illustrated on page 71). Also, speak to antique dealers and ask them to contact you when they have new stock.

A few weeks after I started collecting shoes I decided it would be a good idea to catalog my purchases. I have never regretted this decision and often refer to information on early acquisitions, as this system has proven invaluable to me while updating the first *Shoes of Glass* book. I use 3 x 5 index cards and arrange the information in the following manner:

Catalog #

Good description including length and height.

Where purchased. Name of show or flea market.

Dealer's name, address and phone number.

Date of purchase   Amount paid

This is also a good place to keep notes about the available colors, maker, if reproduced, etc.

DEFINITIONS

There are many stirrup cups shown in the book and, while the definitions in the dictionary are (1) a farewell drink taken by a rider mounting to depart, and (2) any farewell drink, most glass stirrup cups were probably made as whimseys and not used for drinking.

Throughout the book I have used "crystal" to describe color.

While on the subject of definitions I should mention that a vamp is the part of a boot or shoe covering the instep, which is the area between the ankle and the toes. Lastly, a "bootee" refers to a baby's soft-knitted shoe.

Shoes of Glass
~ Book 1 ~

INTRODUCTION TO COLOR PLATES

The original color plates from the first *Shoes of Glass* book have been reproduced here at a larger size, providing for more detail (with the exception of plates 49 through 54 which I have purposely omitted). Individual photos of shoes representing a special color, design or variation are included after their respective plates.

As in the first *Shoes of Glass* book, each illustrated shoe or boot has been given a number, which can be used to reference a description and a value. I have retained the same shoe numbers since they have become a shoe collector's standard, and you will find that additional shoes have been assigned a number followed by a letter, signifying which shoe they represent. For example, shoe (6A) is really shoe (6), but in blue. Shoe (10A) is the same color as shoe (10), but frosted.

Plates 49 through 54 have been omitted altogether because I have not kept up with the new issues of Fenton, Boyd and other companies still making slippers and boots. The omission accounts for the break in shoe numbers which occurs on pages 59 and 94.

PLATE 1 DAISY & BUTTON

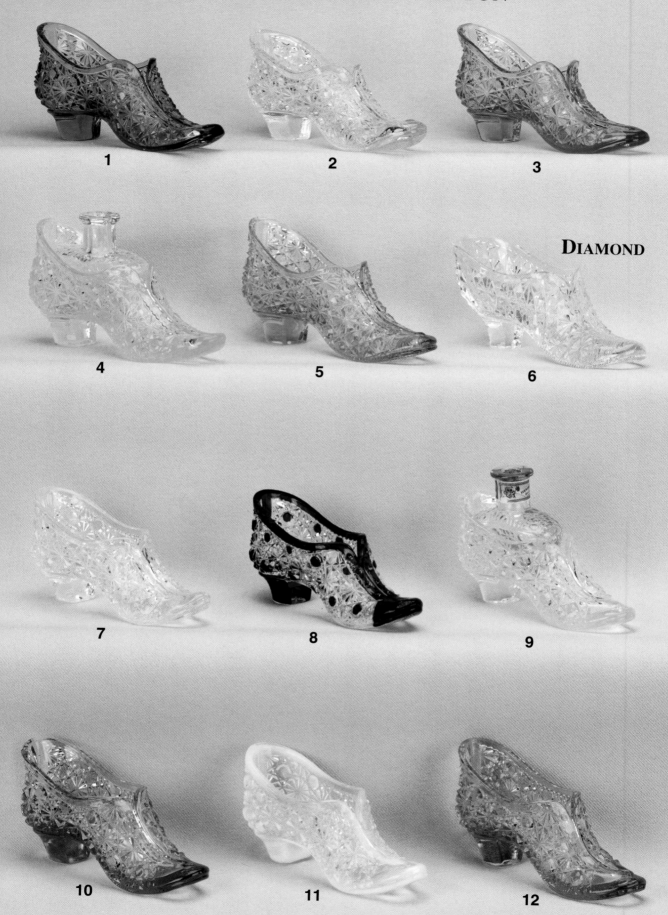

DIAMOND

1

2

3

4

5

6

7

8

9

10

10

11

12

Comparison of shoe (8) and shoe (1A). **(1A)** is the larger of the two, measuring 5³⁄₄" long, 3" high. This shoe is rare and only two are known.

(6A) Same as (6) but in blue. 5³⁄₄" long, 2⁵⁄₈" high.

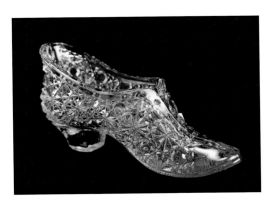

(7A) Same as (7), old gold. 5" long, 2¹⁄₂" high.

(10A) Same as (10), frosted blue. 5" long, 2¹⁄₂" high.

(20A) Same as (20), opaque blue. 4⁷⁄₈" long, 2³⁄₈" high.

(20B) Same as (20), gold. 4⁷⁄₈" long, 2³⁄₈" high.

PLATE 2 DAISY & BUTTON, FINECUT

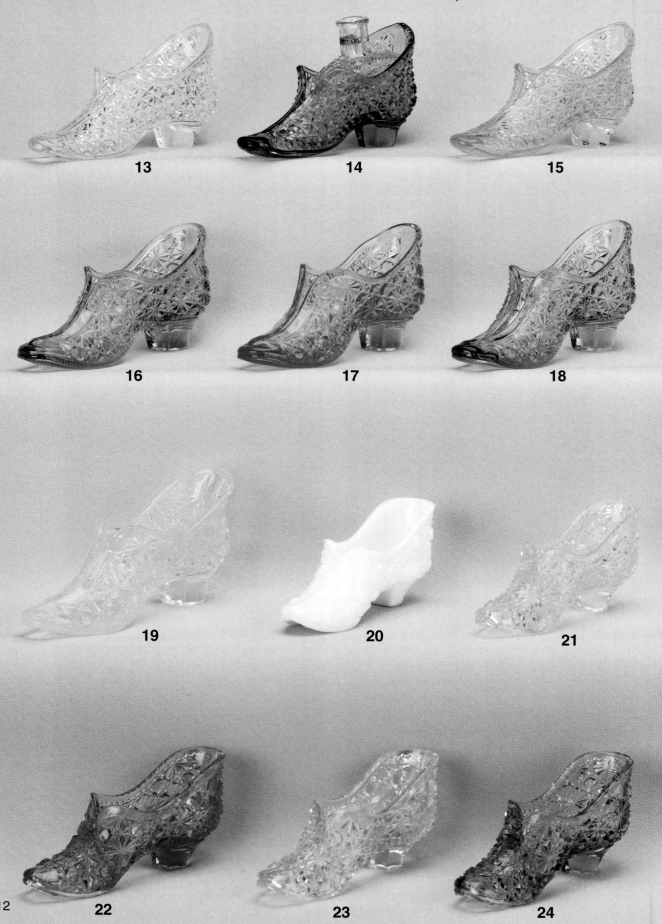

13

14

15

16

17

18

19

20

21

12

22

23

24

PLATE 3 DAISY & BUTTON, DAISY

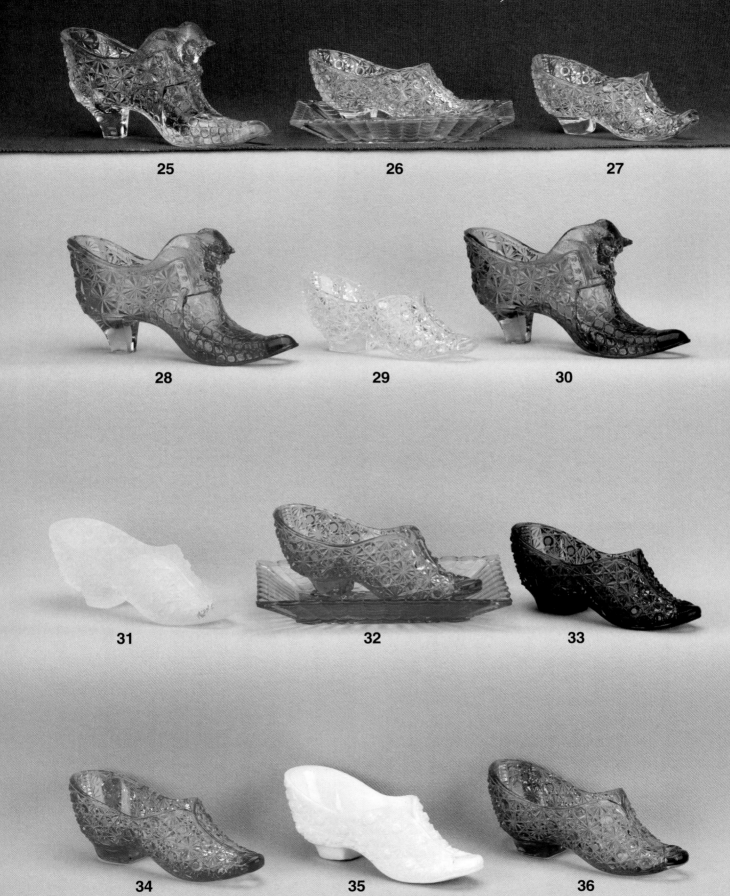

25

26

27

28

29

30

31

32

33

34

35

36

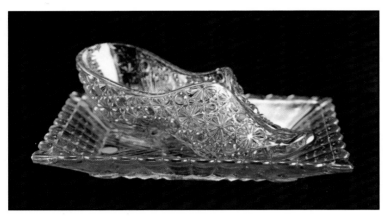

(26A) Overall size of the tray is 5³/₈" long by 4" wide. Same as (26), amber.

(26B) Overall size of the tray is 5³/₈" long by 4" wide. Vaseline, rare for this shoe on the tray.

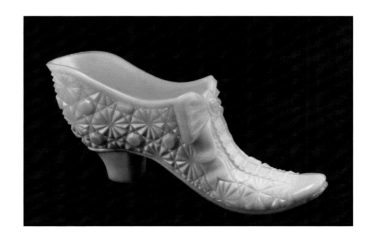

(37A) Same as (37), opaque blue. 5³/₄" long, 2¹/₂" high.

(27A) Same as (27), in crystal decorated with gold. 4⁵/₈" long, 1⁷/₈" high.

PLATE 4 DAISY & BUTTON, DIAMOND

37   38   39

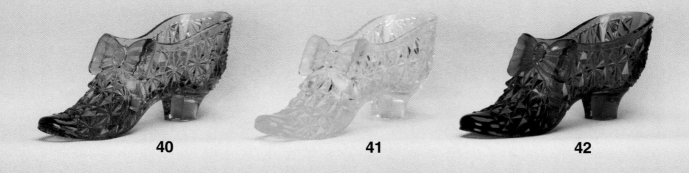

40   41   42

43   44   45

46   47   48

PLATE 5 FINECUT, DAISY & BUTTON

49   50   51

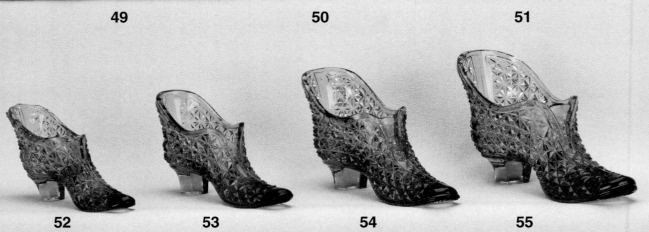

52   53   54   55

56   57   58   59

60   61   62   63

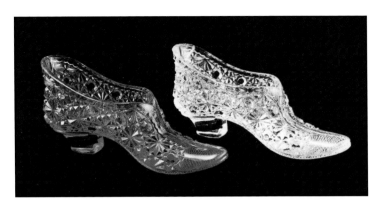

(60A) (60B) Same as (60), in blue and crystal. 4⁷/₈" long, 2¹/₂" high.

(62A) Same as (62), in amber. This shoe is rare in any color. 3" high, 4³/₈" long.

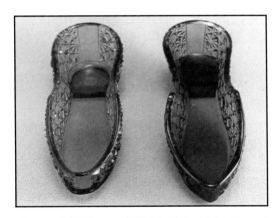

Comparison of (76) and (76A). What I believe to be the original mould is on the left (76), and the later one with the more pointed toe and wider in the front is on the right (76A), amethyst.

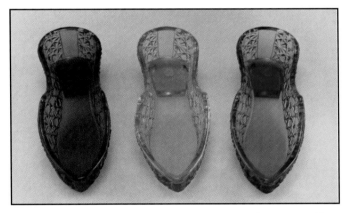

(76A) Amethyst, (75A) amber, (64A) green. The above three sandals have the pointed toe and wider front. All are L. G. Wright shoes, 4⁵/₈" long, 1¹/₂" high.

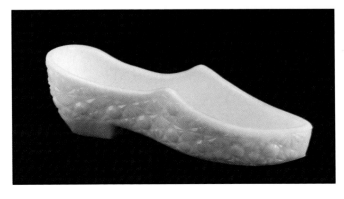

(76B) Opaque white. This color and the green in (64A) are not known in the original mould with the rounder toe. L. G. Wright shoe, 4⁵/₈" long.

PLATE 6 Cane, Daisy & Button

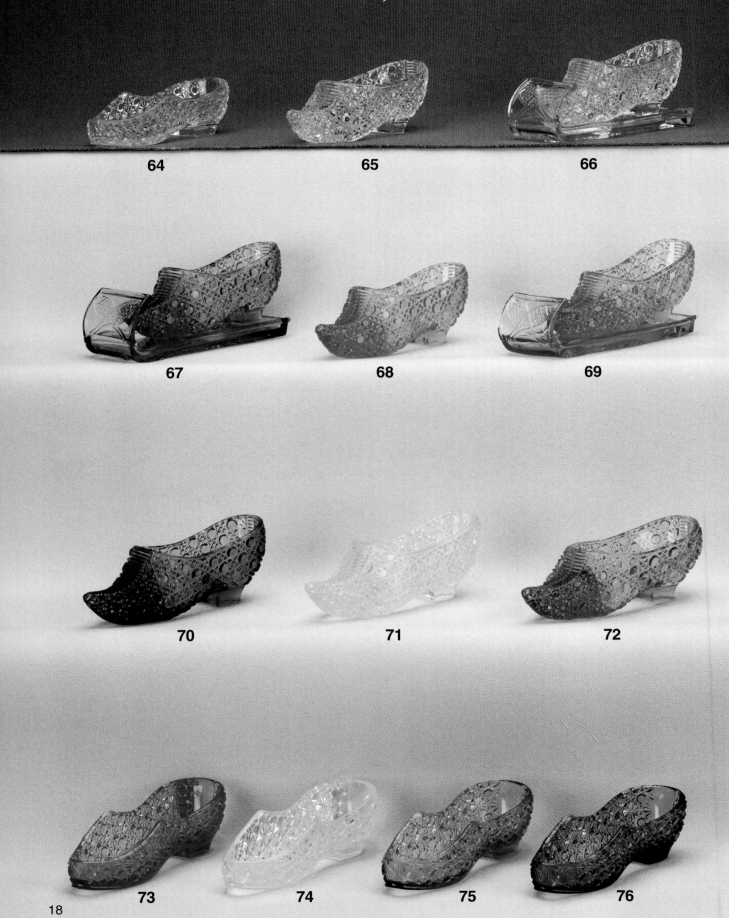

64

65

66

67

68

69

70

71

72

73

74

75

76

PLATE 7 PRESSED SHOES AND BOTTLES

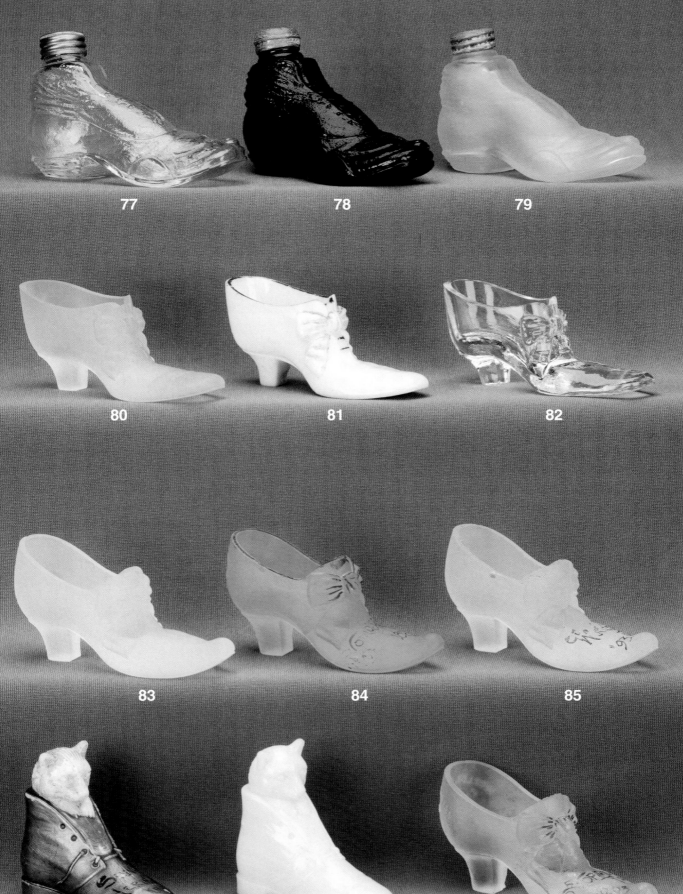

77

78

79

80

81

82

83

84

85

86

87

88

19

(78A) Same as (78) but the left toe, which is showing through the shoe, has been painted a very natural-looking flesh color. 5³/₄" long, 4¹/₄" high.

(82A) Same as (82) but painted black and containing a pincushion. Shoes dating back to the turn of the Century often contained pincushions, probably because so many women did their own sewing and mending. 5³/₄" long, 2¹/₂" high.

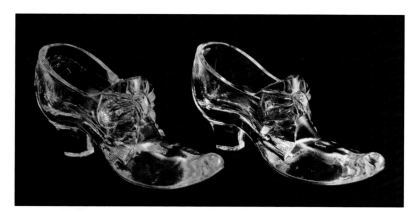

(84A) (83A) Vaseline—either frosted or clear—and clear crystal are scarce colors for this shoe, which is generally found in frosted crystal. Both 4⁷/₈" long, 2³/₄" high.

(88A) Same as (84). Frosted crystal with embossed lettering on the back, that reads WORLD'S COLUMBIAN EXPOSITION 1893.

PLATE 8   GILLINDER, SOWERBY

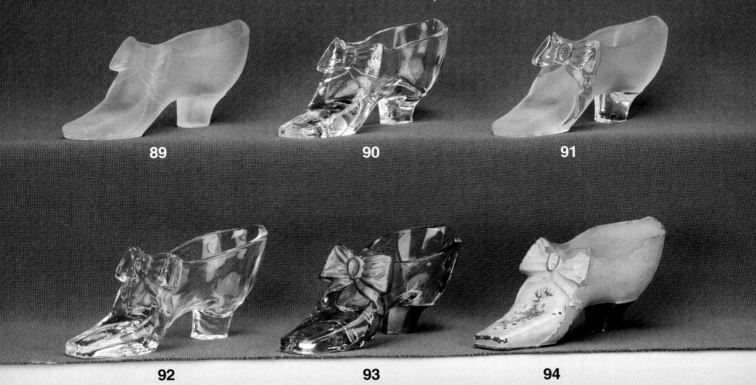

89   90   91

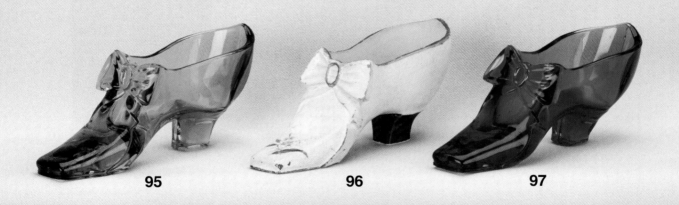

92   93   94

95   96   97

98   99   100

(89A) Frosted crystal Gillinder with hand-painted flowers on the front and sides of the shoe. 5$\frac{1}{2}$" long, 2$\frac{5}{8}$" high.

(99A) Sowerby shoe, same as (99) but with much better color. 5$\frac{7}{8}$" long, 2$\frac{1}{2}$" high.

(103A) Same as (103), in crystal. 2$\frac{5}{8}$" high, 2$\frac{3}{4}$" long.

(99B) Sowerby shoe, same as (99), in turquoise slag, a scarce color. **(98A)** Same as (98), teal. Both 5$\frac{7}{8}$" long, 2$\frac{1}{2}$" high.

(104A) Vaseline, a scarce color for this shoe. 4$\frac{3}{4}$" long, 1$\frac{3}{4}$" high.

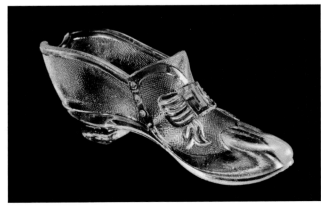

Comparison of the different heels and top openings of shoes (107A) and (108).
(107A) dips down on the sides but is high in front. It is the same as (107) with a differently shaped heel that flares out. **(108)** has a V-front and a straight heel. Both are 4⁵/₈" long, 2¹/₄" high.

(109A) Same as (109), vaseline.
3¹/₈" high, 3" long.

(109B) Same as (109), blue.
3¹/₈" high, 3" long.

PLATE 9 PRESSED SHOES AND BOOTS

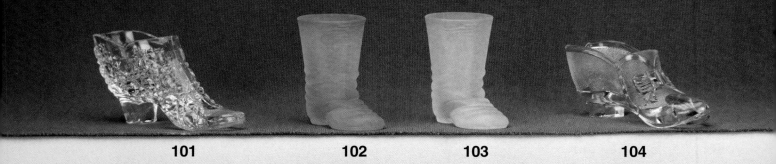

101   **102**   **103**   **104**

105   **106**   **107**

108   **109**   **110**   **111**

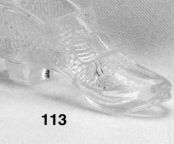

112   **113**   **114**

PLATE 10 PRESSED SHOES

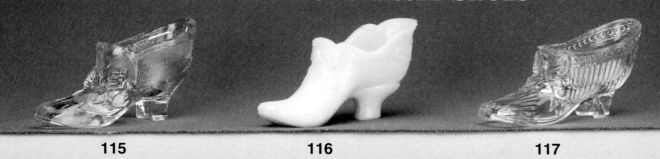

115   **116**   **117**

118   **119**   **120**

121   **122**   **123**

124   **125**   **126**

(115A) (115B) Blue and black.
Both 4⁷/₈" long, 2⁵/₈" high.

(115C) Teal, 4⁷/₈" long, 2¹/₂" high.

(117A) Same as (117), in blue. Sowerby shoe with peacock head mark inside the heel. 4⁷/₈" long, 2³/₈ high.

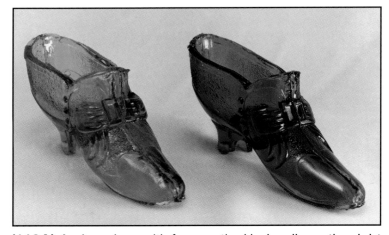

(118A) Amber shoe with four vertical hobnails on the right side. 4³/₄" long, 2¹/₂ high. **(118B)** Blue shoe with four vertical hobnails on the right side. 4³/₄" long, 2¹/₂ high.

(118C) Same shoe as (118), in blue opalescent. Opalescence is unusual for this mould. 4³/₄" long, 2¹/₂" high. Photo courtesy of Mr. Denis Doll.

(119A) (119B) Both same as (119), black with scalloped top edge. (119A) is 4³/₄" long, 2¹/₂" high, while (119B) is 4³/₄" long, 2³/₈" high, and has a pincushion, popular during the Victorian era.

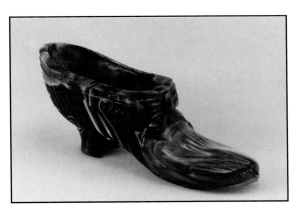

(124) Purple/white slag shoe. 5" long, 2³/₈" high.

(136A) Same as (136), black. This boot has both the thumbprint indentation and a chevron on the sole. Measures 3¹/₄" high, 4" long including spur.

(127A) Same as (127), in old gold. 4¹/₄" high, 4³/₄" long.

PLATE 11 PRESSED BOOTS

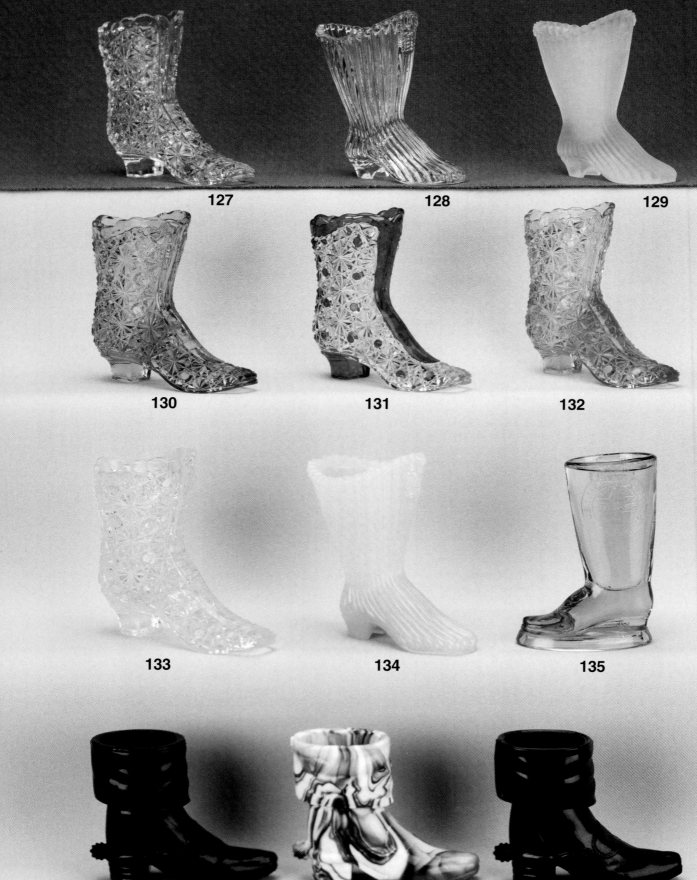

127

128

129

130

131

132

133

134

135

136

137

138

PLATE 12 PRESSED BOOTS

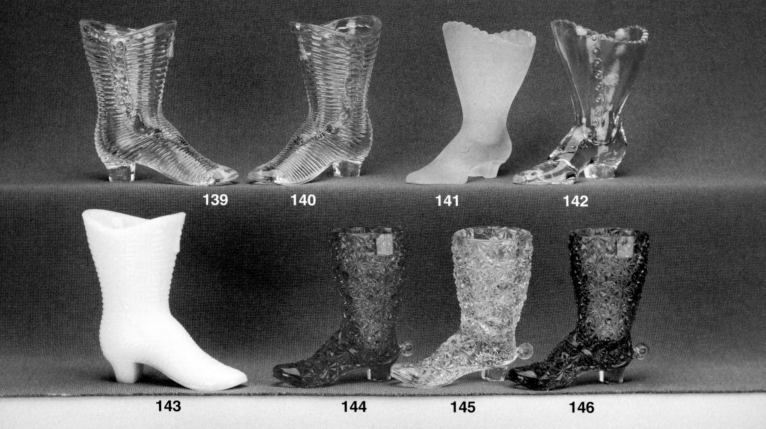

139   140   141   142

143   144   145   146

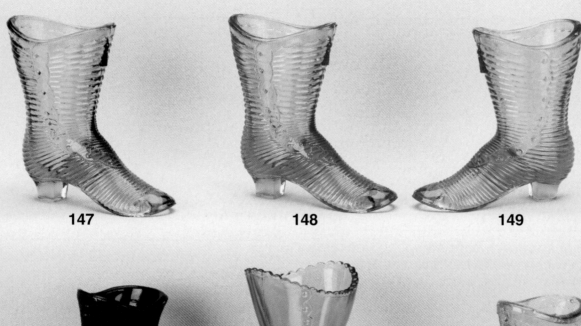

147   148   149

150   151   152

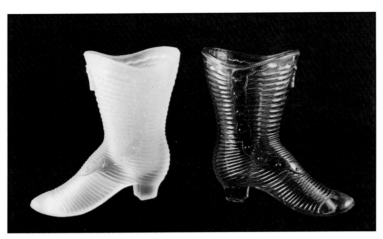

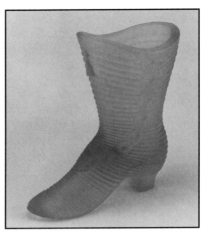

(140A) Frosted crystal boot with buttons on the left side. **(139A)** Green boot with buttons on the right side. Both 4¹/₄" high, 4¹/₄" long.

(147A) Same as (147), frosted amber, with buttons on the left side. 4¹/₄" high, 4¹/₄" long.

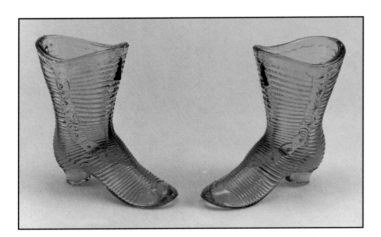

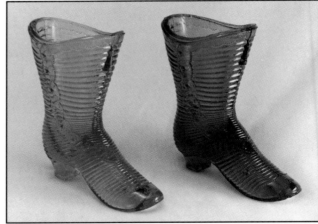

(147) Amber shoe with buttons on the right side. **(147B)** Amber shoe with buttons on the left side. Together, they make a very nice pair. Both 4¹/₄" high, 4¹/₄" long.

(148) This shoe is the usual shade of blue found for this mould. **(148A)** Same shoe in an unusual shade of blue, with buttons on the right. Both 4¹/₄" high, 4¹/₄" long.

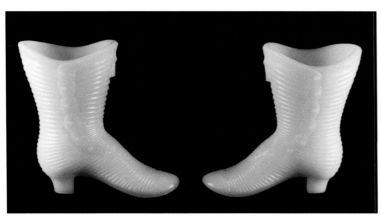

(143) Opaque white high shoe with buttons on the right.
(143A) Opaque white high shoe with buttons on the left.
Both 4¼" high, 4¼" long.

(150A) Same as (150), in dark blue.
Probably English. 3⅝" high, 4⅛" long.

(161A) Same as (161), in crystal.
4" long, 3" high.

(161B) Same as (161), in amber.
4" long, 3" high.

PLATE 13 PRESSED ROLLER SKATES

153   154   155   156

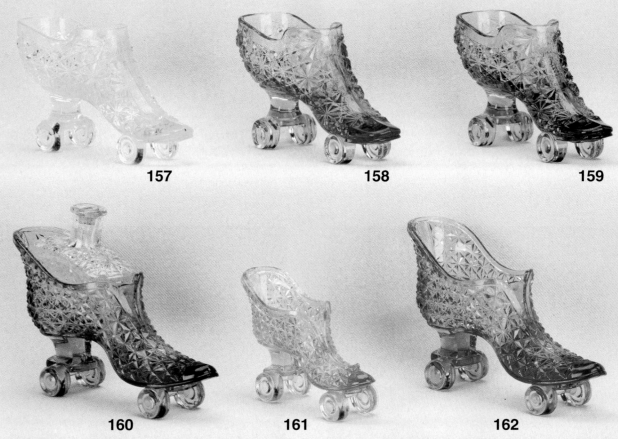

157   158   159

160   161   162

163   164   165   166

PLATE 14 DIAMOND BLOCK, DIAMOND MESH

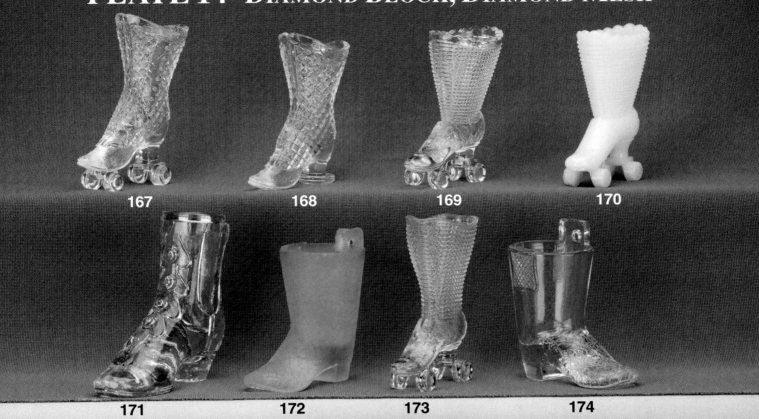

167 168 169 170

171 172 173 174

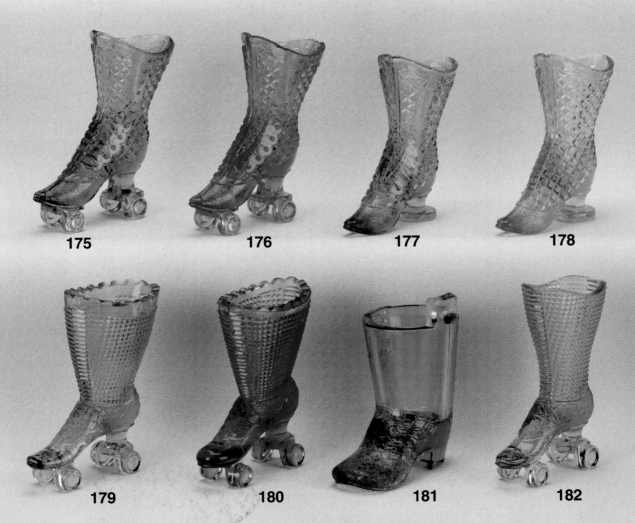

175 176 177 178

179 180 181 182

(168) The important and unique thing about this boot is the bottle. It fits into the shoe perfectly and the Diamond pattern on the bottom portion of the bottle is exactly the same as the Diamond pattern on the shoe. This is the very first known bottle with matching shoe. The bottle is 2³/₄" high.

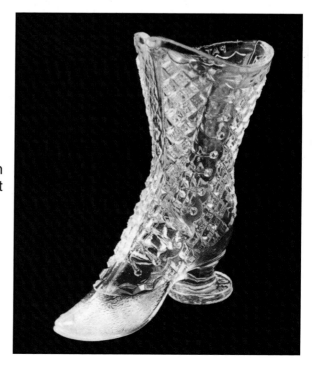

(177A) One of only two known Herman Tappan shoes with the heelplate, in vaseline. Buttons on the left side, patent date on the top edge, right side. 4¹/₈" high, 3³/₄" long.

(169A) Same as (169), in blue. 4" high, 3½" long.

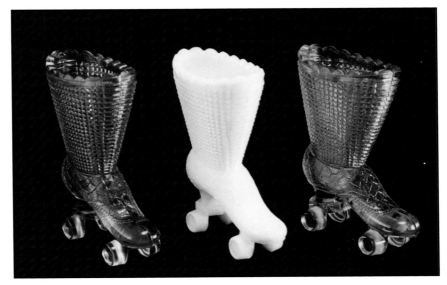

(170A) (170B) (170C) These skates in blue, opaque white and amber are the same as (170), and are marked BOTTLE MADE IN FRANCE. All 4" high, 3¼" long.

(172A) Same as (172), blue. 4" high to top of tab, 3⅜" long.

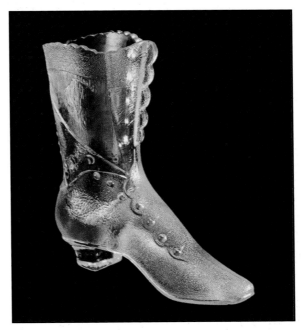

(192A) Same as (192), vaseline. 5" high, 5" long.

PLATE 15 FINECUT, STIPPLED

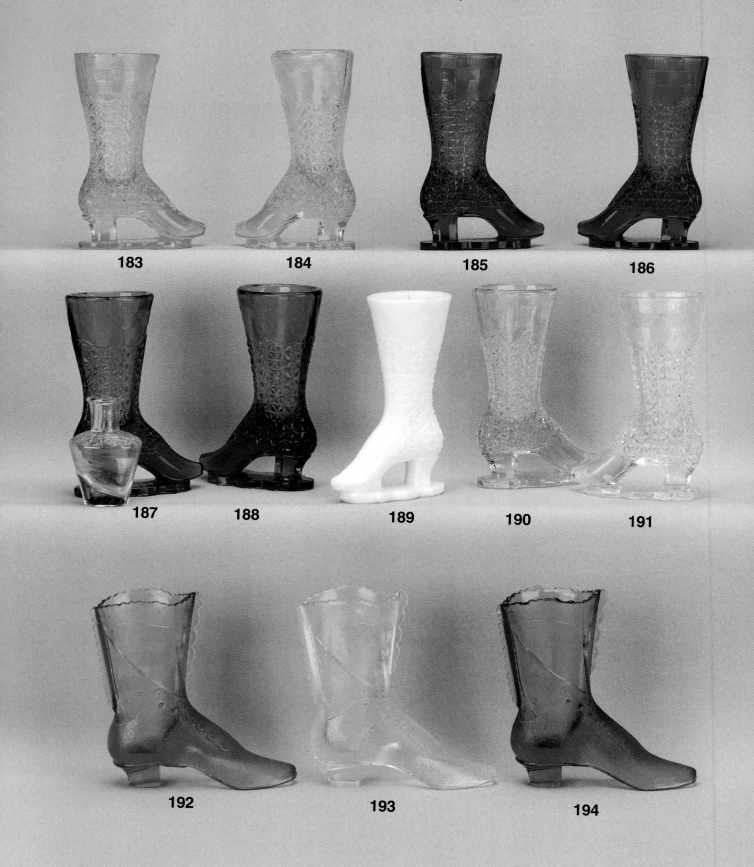

183

184

185

186

187

188

189

190

191

192

193

194

PLATE 16 PRESSED AND BLOWN BOOTS

195

196

197

198

199

200

201

202

(196A) Dark blue blown boot that is similar to (196). 6³/₈" high, 5" long.

(196B) Dark green blown boot, also similar to (196). 6" high, 5¹/₈" long.

(198A) (198B) Similar to (198), the crystal boot on the left has three hand-painted scenes of Kiel, Germany. The boot on the right shows a town and large church in Freiburg, Germany. Both 6¹/₂" high, 4³/₄" long.

(202A) 5¹/₂" high, 5¹/₄" long. Same as (202), this amber boot is the only one I know of from this mould.

(204A) A more colorful version of (204). The vial holders are blue and opaque white; the glass flowers are pink. 5" high.

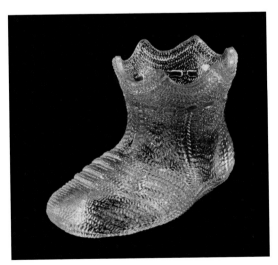

(207A) Same as (207), apple green. Made by the King Glass Co. of Pittsburgh (seen in Figure 15). 2⁵/₈" high, 3⁵/₈" long.

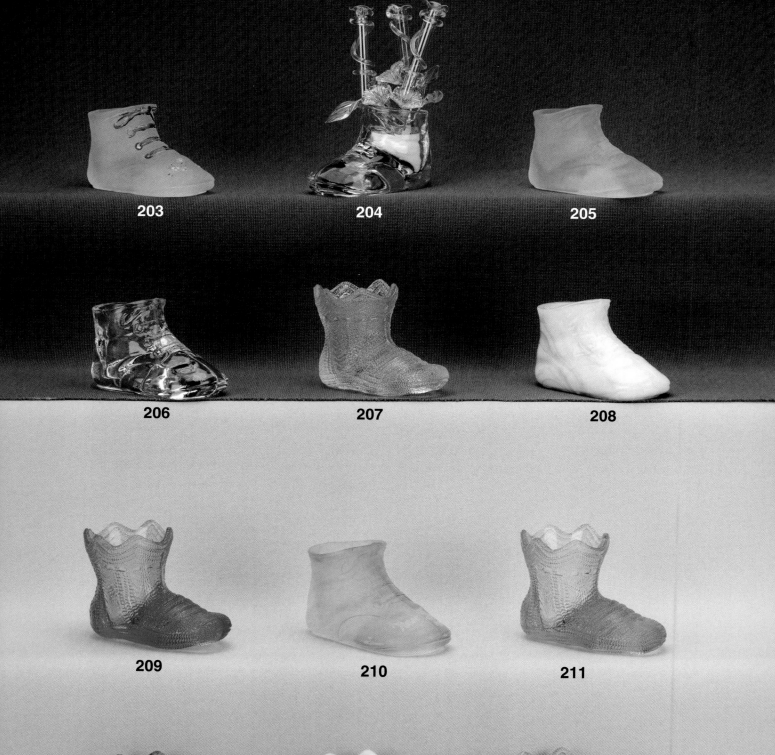

203

204

205

206

207

208

209

210

211

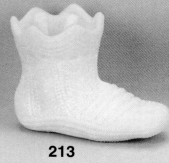

212

213

214

PLATE 18 DIAMOND BOOTEES

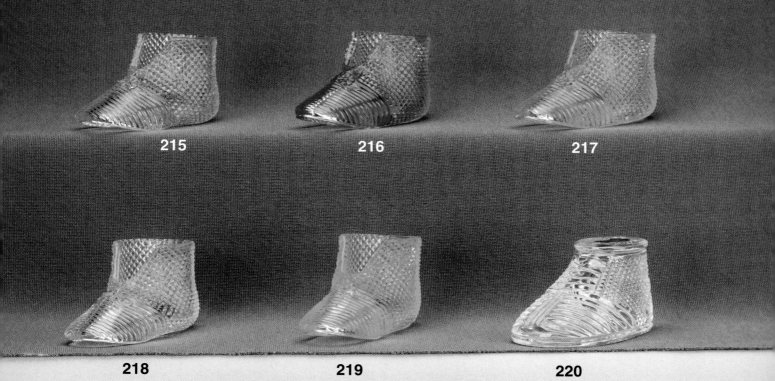

215   **216**   **217**

218   **219**   **220**

221   **222**   **223**

224   **225**   **226**

PLATE 19 PRESSED BOOTEES

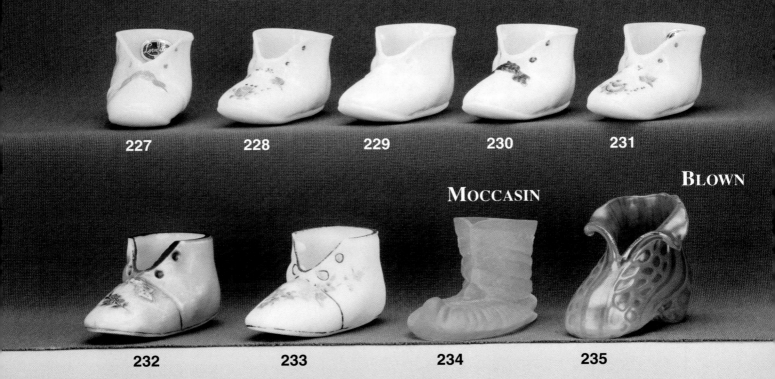

227   228   229   230   231

MOCCASIN   BLOWN

232   233   234   235

236   237   238   239

240   241   242

(233A) Similar to (233), covered with bright, hand-painted flowers. 4" long, 2¼" high.

(235A) Same bootee as (235) but with iridescent amethyst, green, blue and gold. 4" long, 3" high.

This view of the bottom of the rare crystal Duncan bootee (240A) shows that the Duncan toe area comes to a point. **(240A)** Crystal Duncan bootee. 4¼" long, 2⅜" high.

(243A) Gold boot jar, same as (243), but without the lid. 2½" high.

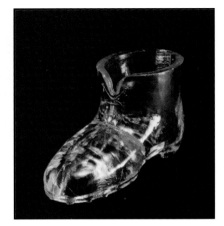

(248A) Same as (248), vaseline. 3⅞" long, 2⅛" high.

(248B) Same as (248). Man's shoe in opaque white, with handpainted flowers. 3⅞" long, 2⅛" high.

(255A) (255B) Same as (255), in opaque blue and blue. These boots have a finely stippled background, and a vine and leaf design. Both boots are 4¼" high, 3½" long.

(257A) Same as (257), in dark green with a silver band around the top. **(255c)** Same as (255), but a smoky color. Both are 4¼" high, 3½" long.

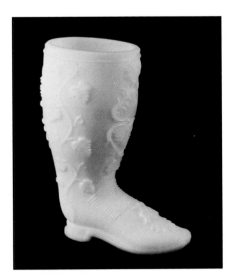

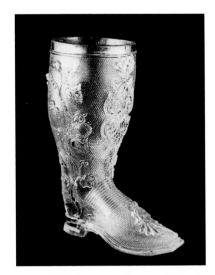

(255D) Same as (255), opaque white. 4¼" high, 3½" long.

(255E) Similar boot to (255), but with a hollow foot as opposed to a solid one. Opalescent. 4½" high, 3⅜" long.

(255F) Also similar to (255), with a hollow foot. Crystal. 4½" high, 3⅜" long.

PLATE 20 PRESSED BOOTS

243   **244**   **245**   **246**

247   **248**   **249**   **250**

251   **252**   **253**   **254**

255   **256**   **257**

45

PLATE 21 PRESSED SHOES AND PIPE HOLDERS

258 **259** **260** **261**

262 **263** **264** **265**

266 **267** **268** **269**

270 **271** **272** **273**

(264A) Same as (264), but the metal trim on this shoe is different. 5" long, 2¼" high.

(264B) Same as (264), but in crystal with a fancy bow on the metal trim. 5" long, 2¼" high.

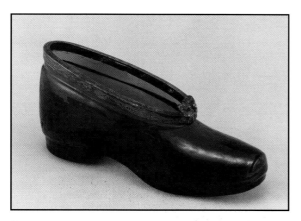

(264C) Same as (264), dark green. 5" long, 2¼" high.

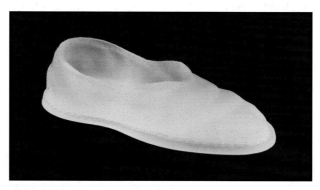

(267A) Same as (267). Frosted crystal man's bedroom slipper, with the following marked on the sole: COMPLIMENTS OF CRESCENT GLASS CO. WELLSBURG, W.VA.

(269A) Same as (269), but with the following marked on the sole: WELLSBURG LODGE NO. 2 AF & AM 1799–1952.

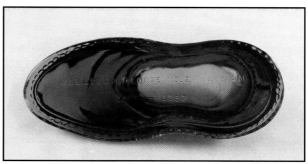

PLATE 22 PRESSED LADIES' SHOES

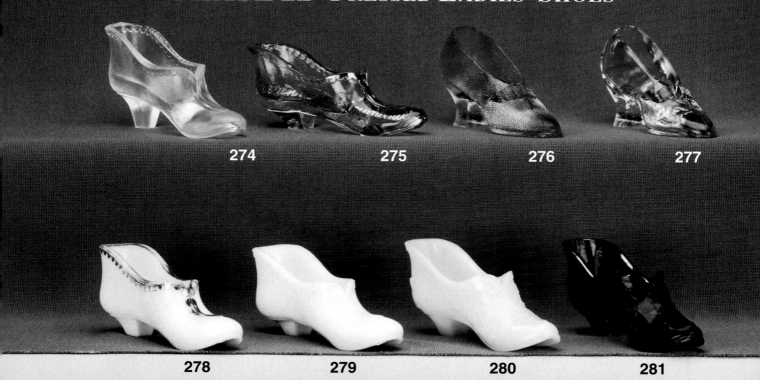

274   275   276   277

278   279   280   281

282   283   284   285

286   287   288

(276A) Same as (276), light marigold carnival. **(277A) (277B)** Same as (277), in amber and painted taupe. All three shoes are 4³/₈" long, 2¹/₂" high.

(279A) Same as (279), opaque white with a greyish cast. 5" long, 2¹/₈" high. **(279B)** Same as (279), opaque white with handpainted flowers all around the shoe. 4⁷/₈" long, 2¹/₈" high.

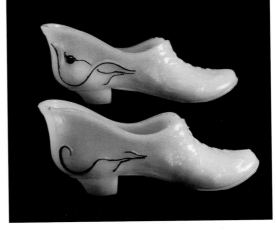

This photograph illustrates the difference between **(286A)**—same as (286) but in opaque white—and **(280)**. Only the trailing vines are different. Each shoe is 5" long and 2¹/₈" high.

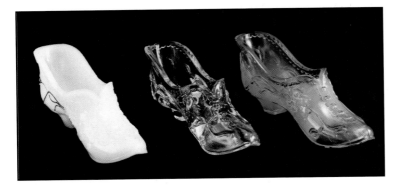

(286A) (286B) (286C) Same as (286), in opaque white, crystal, amber opalescent.

(285A) Same as (285), with DAUGHTER etched on the left side. 4³/₄" long, 2⁵/₈" high.

PLATE 23 BOOTS AND STIRRUPS

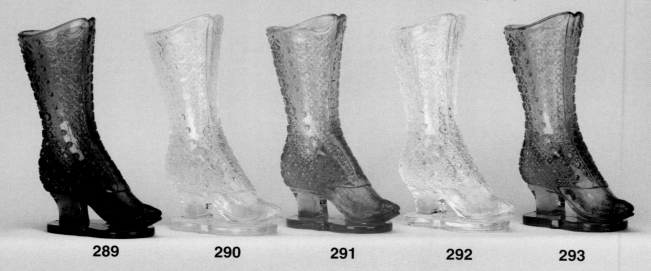

289   290   291   292   293

SOUVENIR SHOES

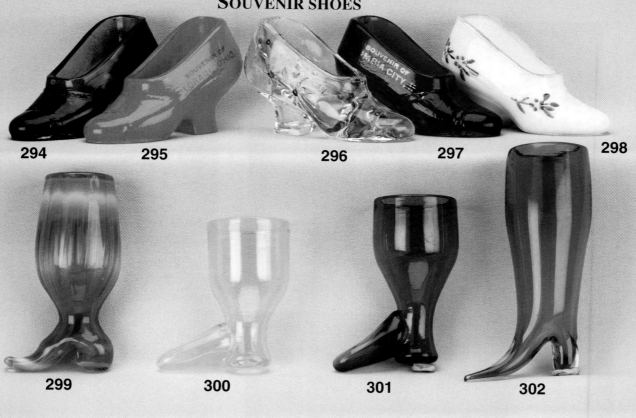

294   295   296   297   298

299   300   301   302

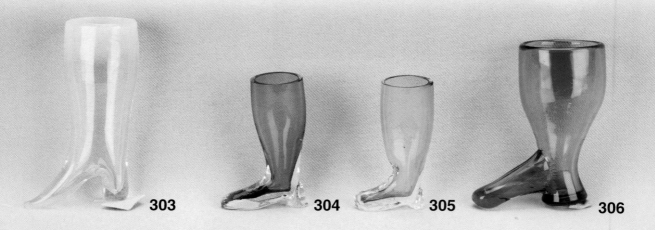

303   304   305   306

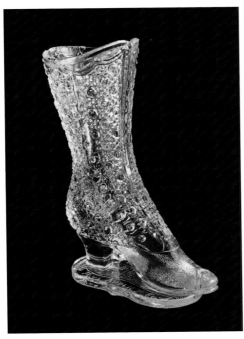

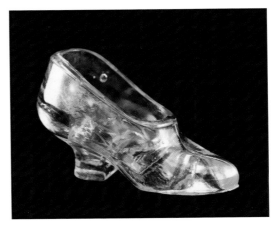

(294A) Same as (294), iridized a light marigold carnival. 4³/₈" long, 2⁷/₈" high.

(289A) Same as (289), but in apple green, a rare color for this shoe. 5¹/₂" high, 4³/₈" long.

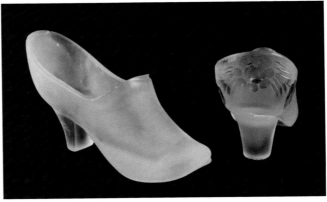

(307) (307A) Frosted crystal. (307A) is the same as (307) with etched design on the back. Both 6³/₈" long, 3¹/₂" high.

(307B) Same as (307), in opaque white with a newer pincushion and trim. 6³/₈" long, 3¹/₂" high.

(308A) Same as (308) in dark blue. This shoe is English and shown on a catalog page from the Burtles, Tate & Company in Manchester, England, c. 1880s.

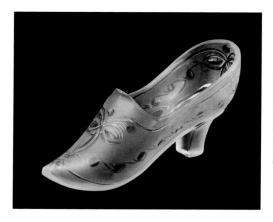

(310A) 6¼" long, 3½" high. Same as (310), this shoe began as crystal, was frosted and then cut back to clear.

(311A) Same as (311) in opaque white with handpainted flowers on the vamp. 6¼" long, 3½" high.

(311B) Same as (311), this opaque white shoe was painted a deep rose on the outside, and covered with handpainted flowers. 6¼" long, 3½" high.

(311C) Same as (311), opaque white and left undecorated. 6¼" long, 3½" high.

(313A) Same as (313) in blue. 4¾" long, 2¼" high.

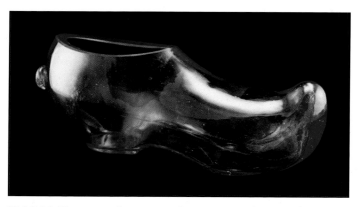

(319A) Green, also seen in crystal. Same as (319) except that there is a small knob on the back of the shoe as shown above. 8¼" long, 3" high.

PLATE 24 PRESSED AND CASED SHOES

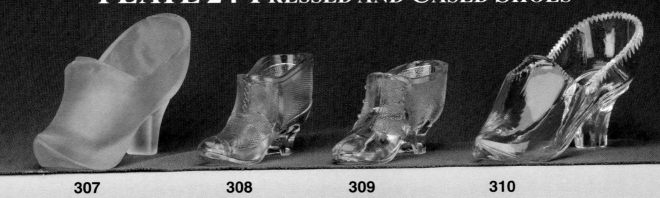

307   **308**   **309**   **310**

311   **312**   **313**   **314**

315   **316**   **317**   **318**

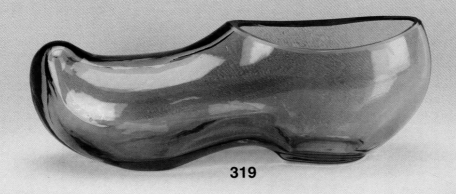

319

PLATE 25 CASED SPATTER BOOTS

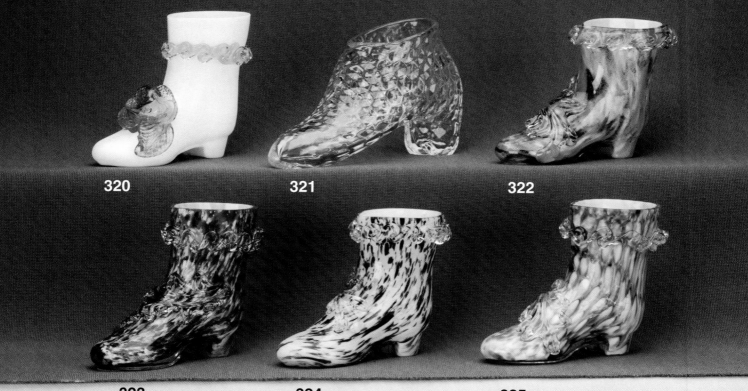

320   **321**   **322**

323   **324**   **325**

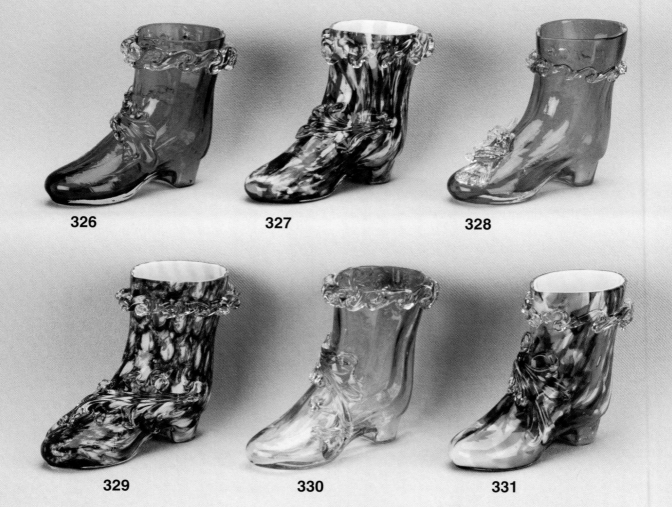

326   **327**   **328**

329   **330**   **331**

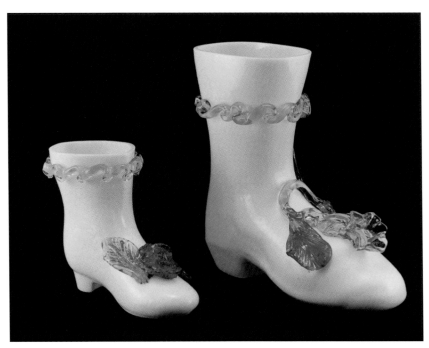

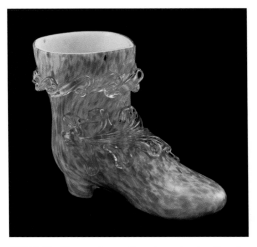

(320) and **(320A)**, both opaque white with amber decorations, but different in size and type of decoration. (320) is 3³/₄" high and 4⁷/₈" long, while (320A) is 6¹/₈" high and 6" long. The smaller boot has a round, layered flower and two leaves, whereas the larger boot has an open, six-pointed flower attached to a stem, which continues to the rigaree at the top.

(324A) Cased spatter boot, similar to (324), in pink, yellow and clear. 3³/₄" high, 5" long.

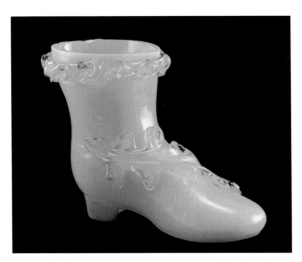

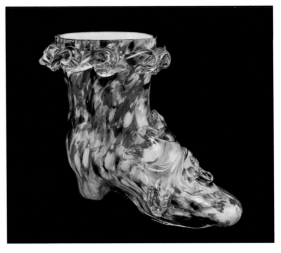

(324B) Cased boot, similar to (324), clear over yellow. 4" high, 5" long.

(327A) Cased spatter boot, similar to (327), in opaque white, red, green, yellow and clear. 3³/₄" high, 5" long.

PLATE 26 CASED SPATTER SHOES

332   333   334

335   336   337

338   339   340

56   341   342   343

(332A) Similar to (332), in opaque white, green and clear; same colors as (325). 5¹/₂" long, 2⁵/₈" high.

(334A) Similar to (334), in opaque white, pink, blue and clear. 5¹/₂" long, 3" high.

(334B) Similar to (334), in opaque white, red, blue and clear. 5¹/₂" long, 3" high.

(334C) Similar to (334), in opaque white, yellow, dark red and clear; same colors as (324). 5¹/₂" long, 3" high.

(339A) Cased shoe in crystal over cranberry. 5³/₈" long, 3¹/₄" high.

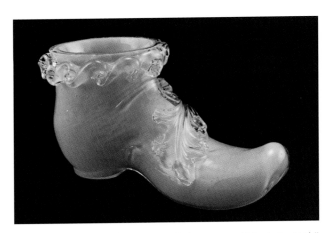

(339B) Cased shoe, crystal over solid pink. 5½" long, 3" high.

(339C) Opaque white shoe with amber rigaree, flower and leaves. 5¼" long, 3⅛" high.

(340A) Similar to (340), in aqua, blue, opaque white, dark red, light olive and clear. 5½" long, 3" high.

(340B) Similar to (340). This shoe is pink on the inside, with dark red, blue, yellow, opaque white and clear. Measures 5½" long, 3" high.

(340C) Similar to (340). Butterscotch color on the inside, with dark red, opaque white, beige and clear. 5⅝" long, 3" high.

PLATE 27 MURANO

344 345 346 347

348 349 350 351

352 353 354 355

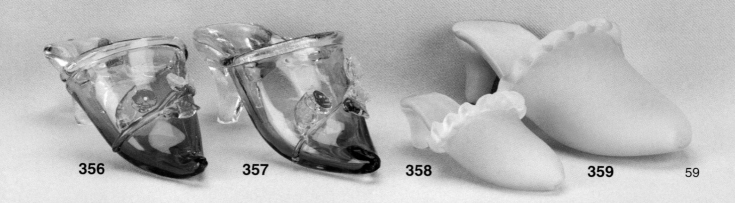

356 357 358 359

(344A) This Millefiore shoe, similar to (344), is unusual because of the black heel and rolled edge. 5¼" long, 3" high.

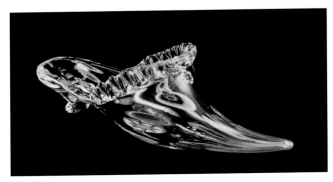

(344B) Crystal shoe with only a few millefiore. 6³/₈" long, 2" high.

(344C) Crystal shoe with three rows of very large millefiore, alternating with rows of twisted blue ribbons. 5¼" long, 1⁷/₈" high.

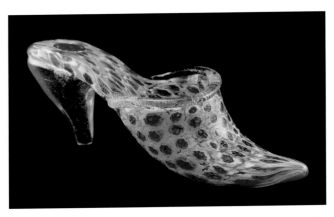

(349A) Similar to (349) but with a rolled front, in green and yellow. There is a red and silver label that reads MURANO GLASS MADE IN ITALY. 6¹/₈" long, 2¼" high.

(345A) Same as (345) but not frosted. Red, white and blue millefiore. 6" long, 1⁷/₈" high.

PLATE 28 MURANO

360   361   362   363   364

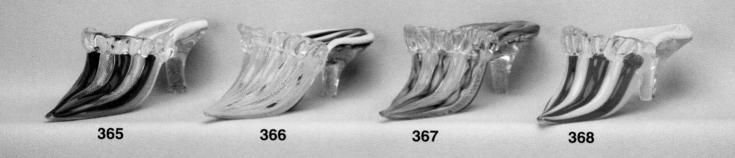

365   366   367   368

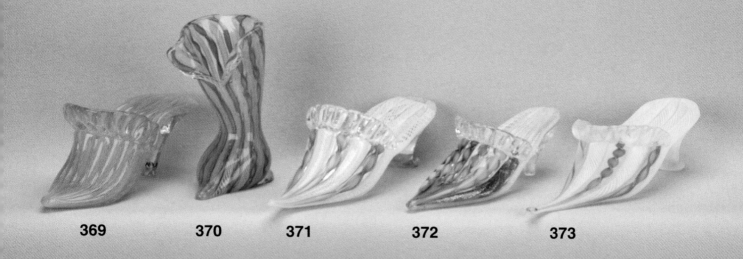

369   370   371   372   373

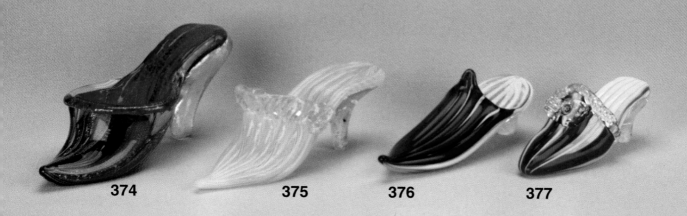

374   375   376   377

PLATE 29 LARGE PRESSED SHOES

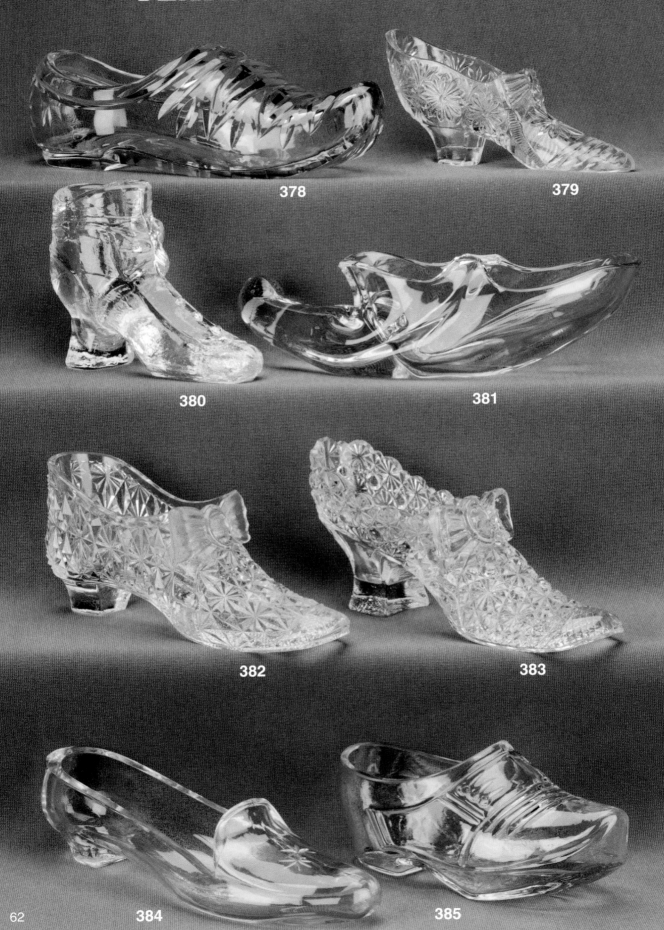

378

379

380

381

382

383

384

385

ADDITIONAL SHOES FOR PLATE 29

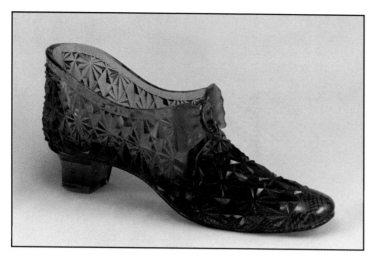

(382A) Same as (382), in amber, but the sole is completely covered with diamond mesh from the tip of the toe to the heel. 8" long, 4" high.

(382B) Exactly the same as (382A), in cobalt. This color is scarce. 8" long, 4" high.

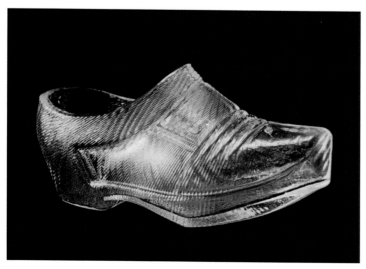

(385A) Same as (385), iridized crystal. 7" long, 3⅛" high.

PLATE 50   ARCHES, DIAMOND, SUNBURST

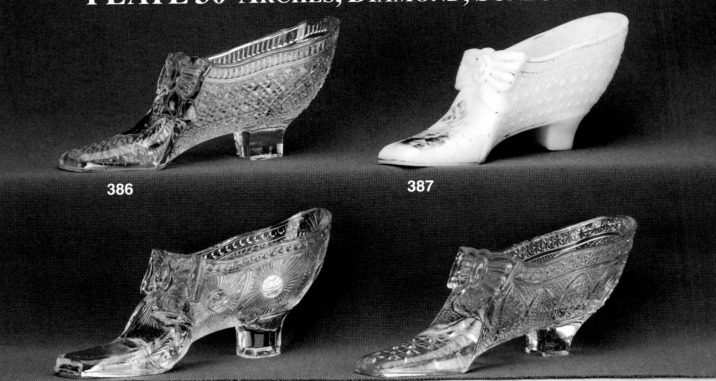

386   **387**

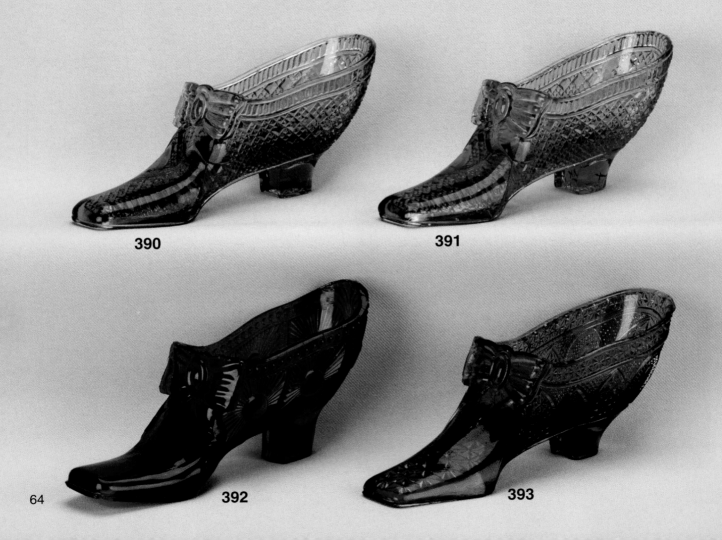

388   **389**

390   **391**

64   **392**   **393**

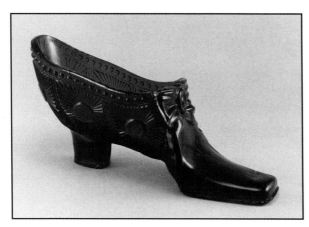

(388A) Same as (388), teal. This shoe has three sunbursts on each side, a hollow sole, indented heel, and Sowerby's embossed peacock head mark on the inside. 7¹/₂" long, 3¹/₂" high.

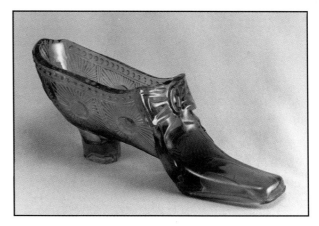

(388B) Same as (388A), amber, including the sunbursts, hollow sole, indented heel and Sowerby's peacock head mark on the inside. 7¹/₂" long, 3¹/₂" high.

(388C) Same as (388A), including the sunbursts, hollow sole, indented heel and Sowerby's peacock head mark on the inside. Purple/white slag. 7¹/₂" long, 3¹/₂" high.

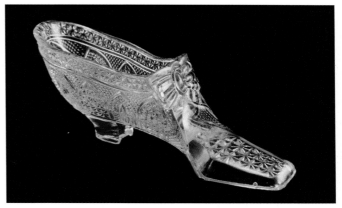

(389A) Same as (389), vaseline. This shoe has arches around the back half and a plain front. Made in Austria. 7⁵/₈" long, 3¹/₈" high.

PLATE 31 MATCH HOLDERS

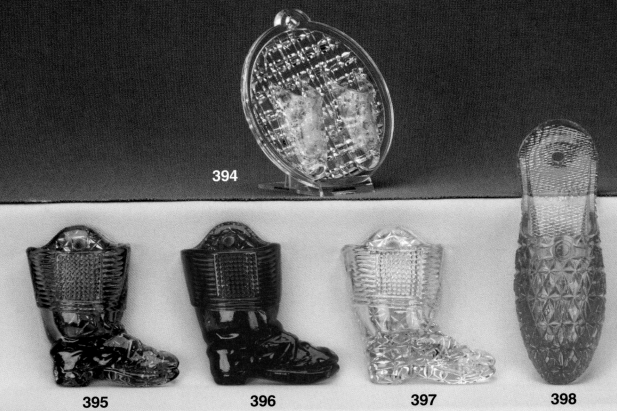

394

395   **396**   **397**   **398**

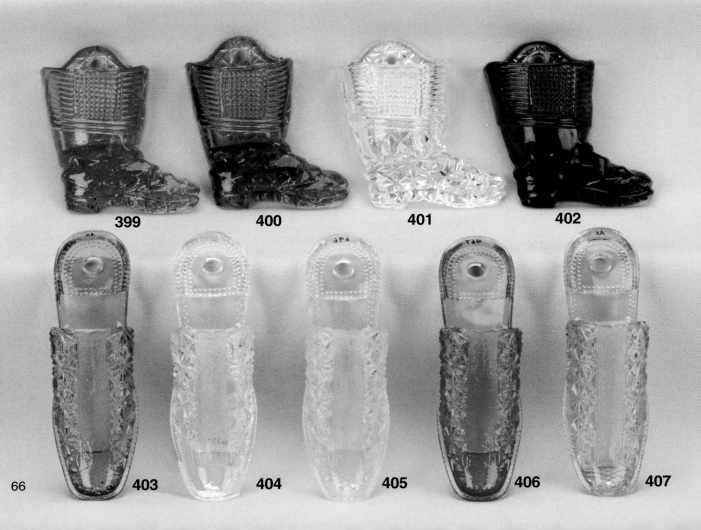

399   **400**   **401**   **402**

403   **404**   **405**   **406**   **407**

(394A) Same as (394), in blue. 4¹/₂" diameter. Here are two views of a round, flat match holder. Two slippers on the front hold the matches, and between them is fine horizontal ribbing for the striker.

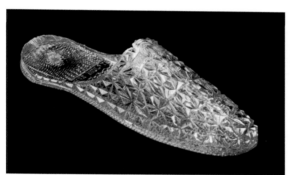

(398A) Same as (398), in amber. 6⁷/₈" long.

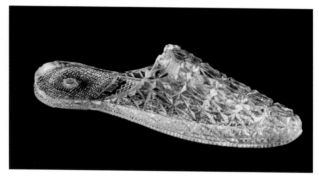

(398B) Same as (398), in crystal. 6⁷/₈" long.

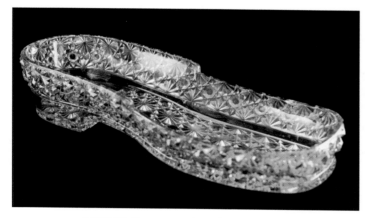

(408A) Same as (408), in amber.
11³/₄" long, 2¹/₂" high, 4¹/₂" wide.

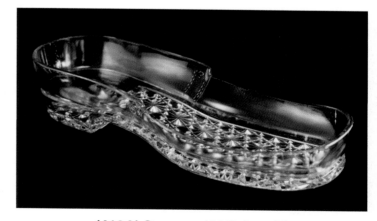

(412A) Same as (412), in gold.
11³/₄" long, 2¹/₂" high, 4¹/₂" wide.

PLATE 32 CELERY HOLDERS

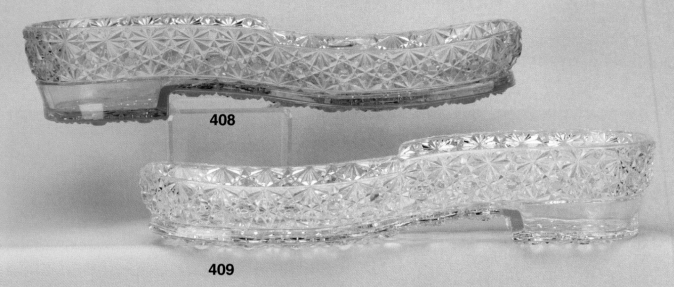

408

409

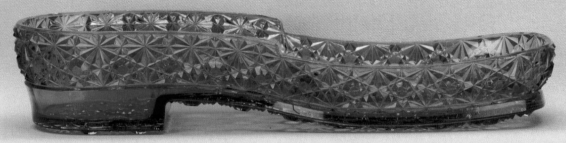

410

411

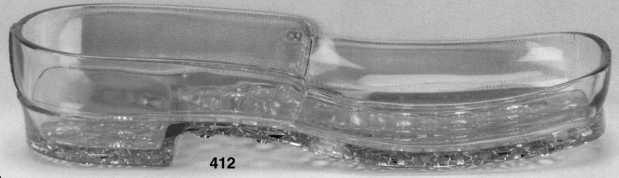

412

PLATE 33 Lamps, Inks and Colognes

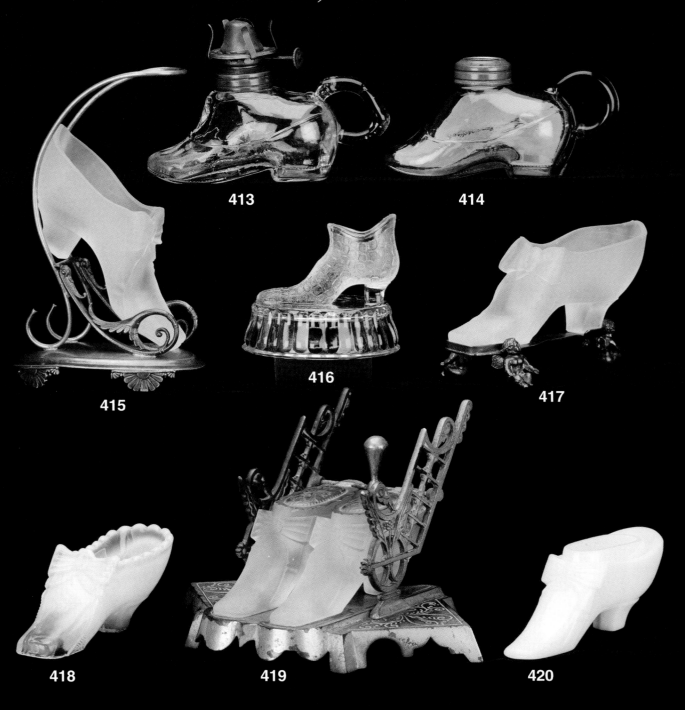

413

414

415

416

417

418

419

420

(413A) Same as (413), blue. 6" long from to to end of handle. 3" high to top of collar.

(413B) Same as (413A), light olive green.

(418A) Same as (418), but in blue opalescent.

(421A) Triple boot match holder, same as (421). Dark amber. 4$\frac{1}{2}$" high, 4$\frac{3}{8}$" wide at the base.

(424A) Similar to (424) but larger and not cut as sharply. 5$\frac{3}{4}$" long, 2$\frac{3}{4}$" high.

PLATE 34 ASSORTED CRYSTAL AND OPAQUE

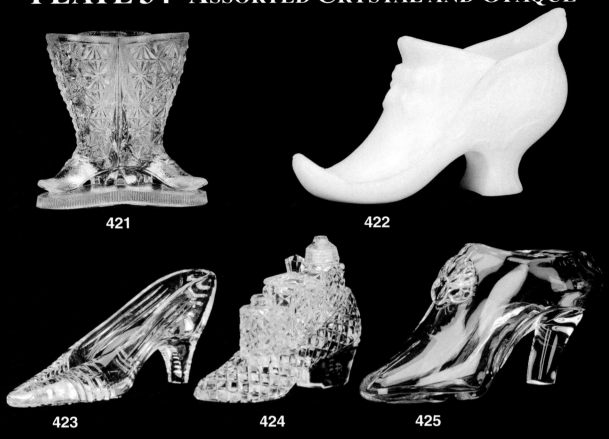

421

422

423

424

425

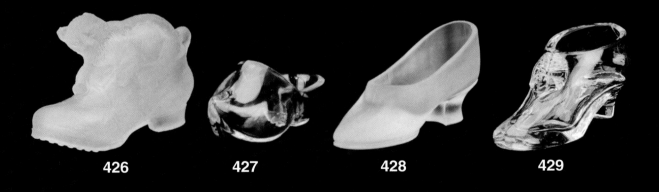

426

427

428

429

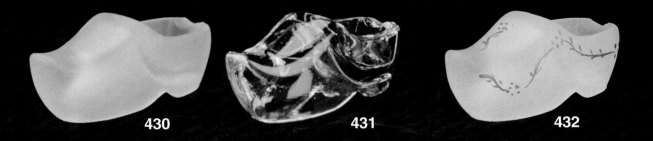

430

431

432

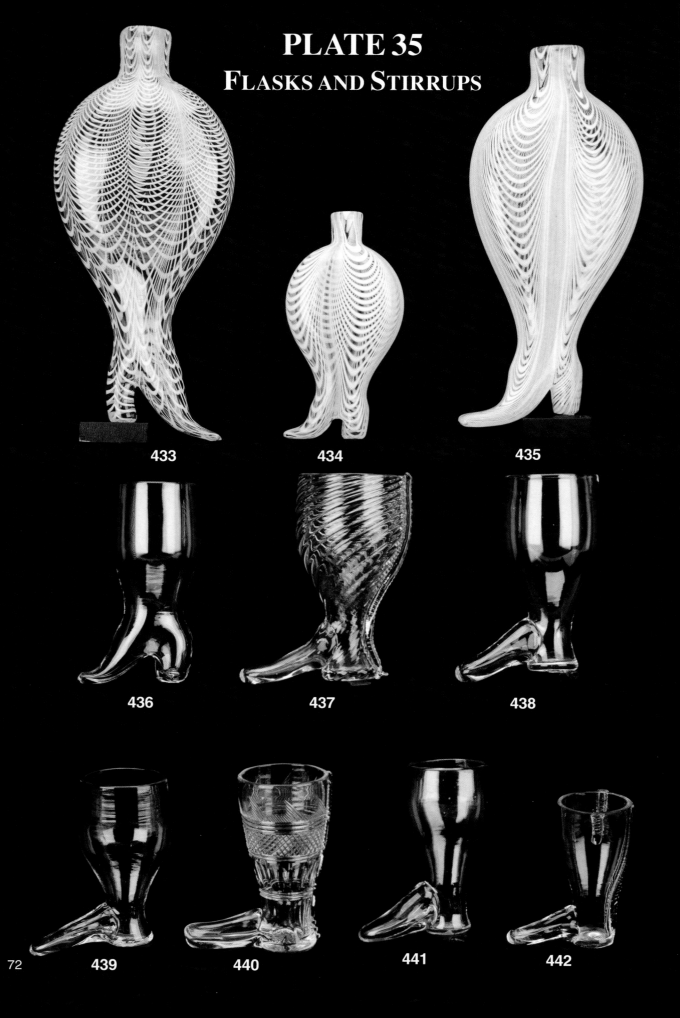

PLATE 35
FLASKS AND STIRRUPS

433

434

435

436

437

438

439

440

441

442

 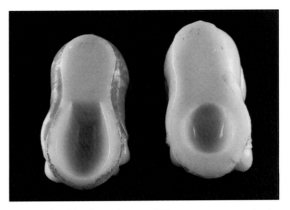

(524) (525) The original tramp shoes are sometimes called baby shoes. They were made in opaque white only, in both the right and left foot. The prominent large toes may be seen in this photograph. Measuring 3" long and 2¹⁄₈" high, the shoes may be found with either a keyhole-shaped depression—such as in (524)—or a round depression in the sole.

(526A) Same bottle as (526), but with different label. 4¹⁄₄" high, 3³⁄₈" long.

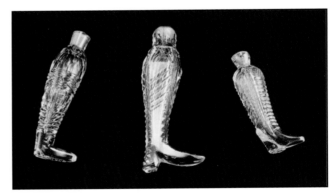

(528A) (528B) (528C) Although all three of these crystal cut-glass boot scent bottles are similar, each one has a different pattern, as do (528–530) and (533).

(533B) Similar to (533). This blue cut glass boot is rare, and measures 2⁵/₈" to top of neck.

(533A) Similar to (533), with silver neck and small crystal stopper. It measures 3¹/₂" to the top of the stopper.

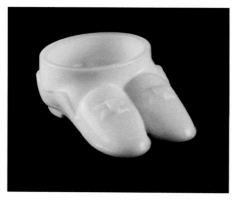

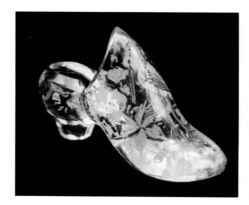

(538A) Same as (538), but in opaque white. 2³/₄" long, 2" wide, 1¹/₄" high.

(542A) Both the side and top views of this shoe show that the original painting is in excellent condition. Same as (542), 2³/₈" long, 1¹/₂" high.

(547A) Blue thimble holder, same as (547). **(547)** Frosted crystal thimble holder with original pincushion. **(547B)** Painted black thimble holder, same as (547). All three measure 3³/₈" long, 1¹/₈" high.

PLATE 41 SMALL BOOTS, BOTTLES AND SHAKERS

550   551   552   553   554

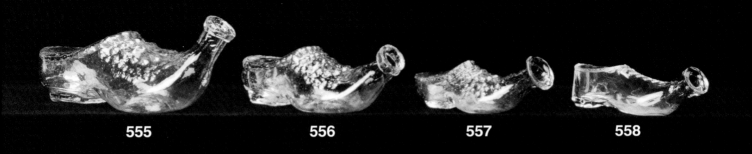

555   556   557   558

559   560   561

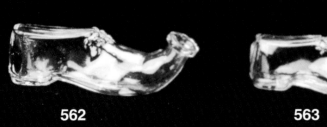

562   563   564

(551A) (551B) Both of these cuffed boots measure 2³/₄" high and 2¹/₂" long, and were made in Finland. Same as (551), in amethyst and cobalt.

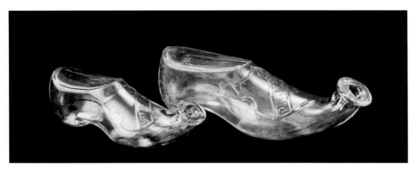

(559A) Similar to (559). 2" long on top, 4⁷/₈" overall length.
(561A) Similar to (561). 2¹/₂" long on top, 5³/₄" overall length. Both of these bottles have an advertisement diagonally across the front which reads PHALON & SON N.Y.

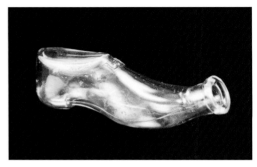

(563A) Similar to (563), with a small buckle and ribbon. 3¹/₂" overall length.

(565A) Same as (565), but etched crystal with matching crystal stems. 15³/₈" high to the top of the cover.

(565B) Same as (565), but in frosted crystal with matching glasses and a silver edge. 15³/₈" high to the top of the cover.

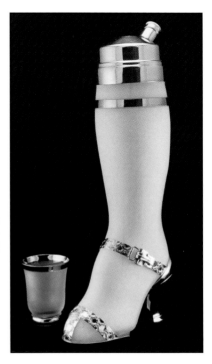

PLATE 42 COCKTAIL SHAKERS AND GLASSES

565

PLATE 43 Boots

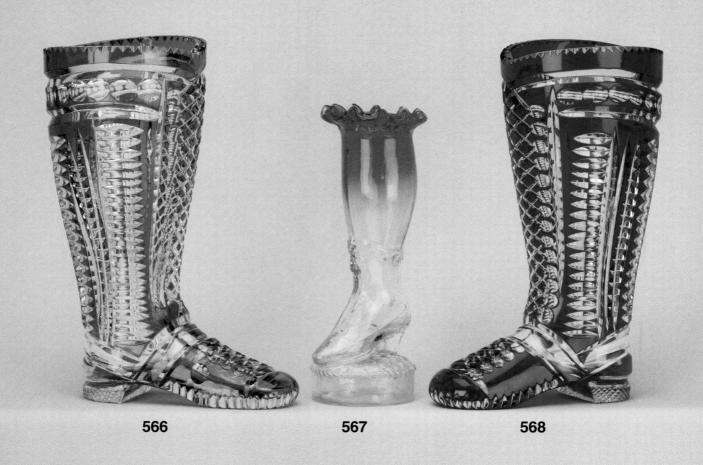

566   **567**   **568**

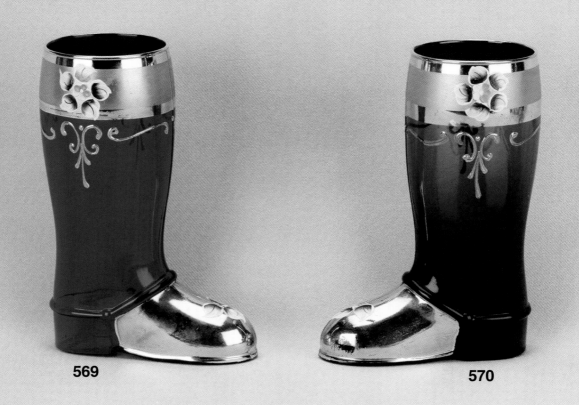

569   **570**

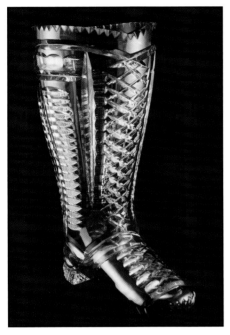

(566A) Same as (566), in green cut back to crystal. Measures 7³/₄" high, 5¹/₂" long.

(569A) Similar to (569), ruby boot decorated with gold and enamel. 6⁷/₈" high, 4³/₄" long.

(569B) Similar to (569) and (570). Smaller ruby boot decorated with gold and enamel. 4³/₈" high, 3¹/₂" long.

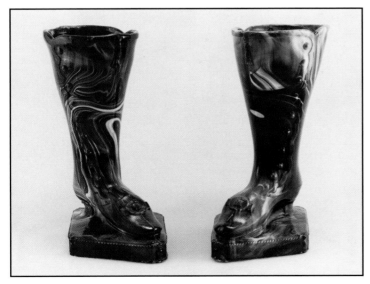

Both boots the same as (574), with buttons on the right **(574A)** and on the left **(574B)**. This pair of purple/white slag ladies' boots are English. 6¹/₂" high, with the base 4¹/₂" long.

(574C) Same as (574). Turquoise/white slag, a rare color in this mould. 6¹/₂" high, with the base 4¹/₂" long.

PLATE 44 Boots

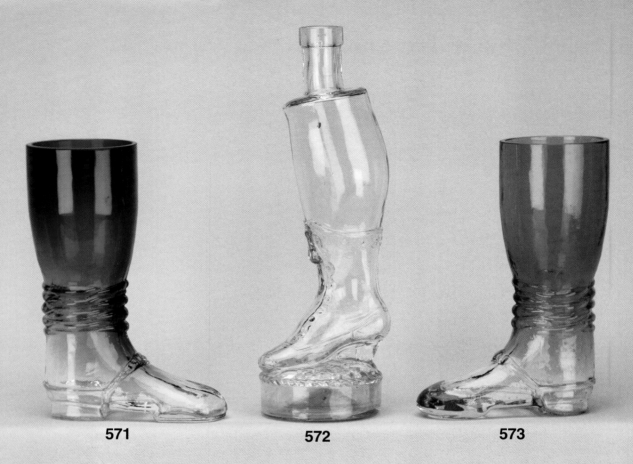

571 **572** **573**

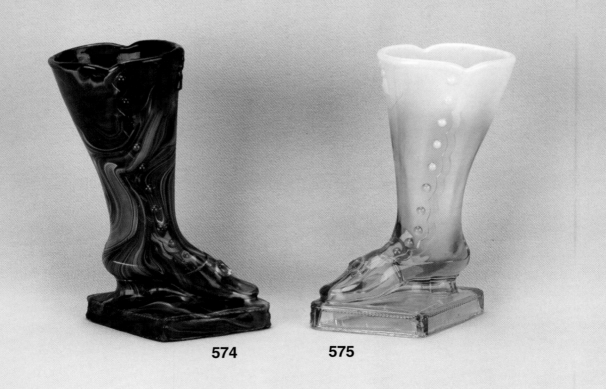

574 **575**

PLATE 45
TALL BOOTS

576

577

578

579

PLATE 46
TALL BOOTS

580

581

90

582

583

584

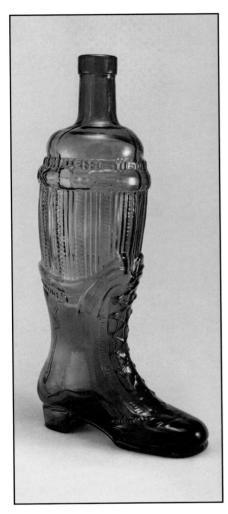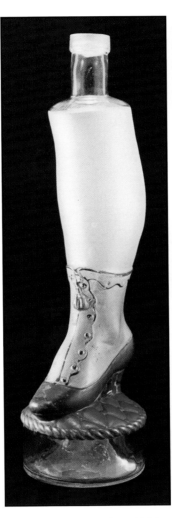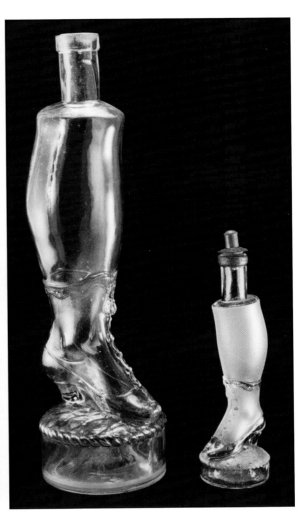

(580A) Green boot bottle. Same as (580), 12¼" high, 6⅜" long. **(581A)** Same as (581). This painted crystal boot bottle measures 15" high to the top and 13" high to the bottom of the neck. Both of these boot bottles are the same as (581). **(581B)** 15" high to the top, 13" high to the bottom of the neck. **(581C)** This boot has its original stopper, and is marked BRADLEY PERFUMERY, N.Y. 6¼" high to the bottom of the neck. Hassock is 2¼" in diameter. (581) and (581C) are the tallest and shortest of these bottles found to date.

PLATE 47 TALL AND MEDIUM BOOTS

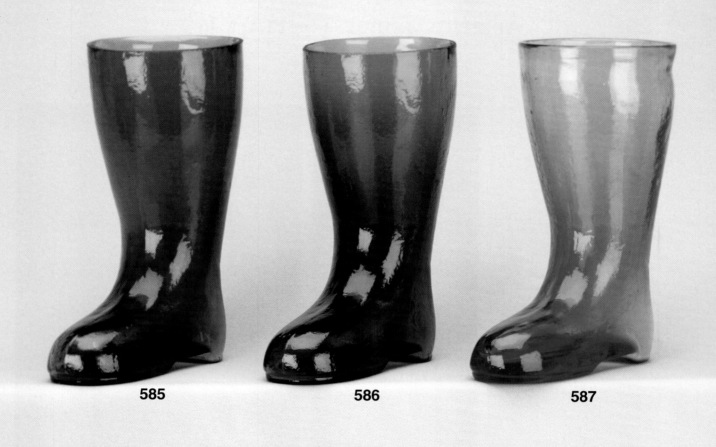

585   **586**   **587**

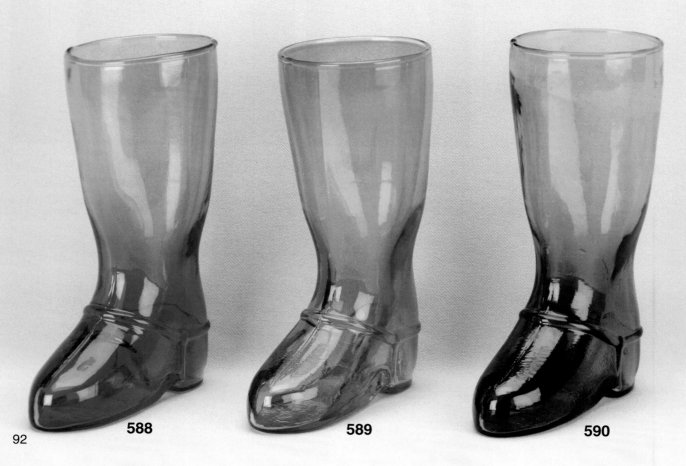

588   **589**   **590**

PLATE 48 Boots

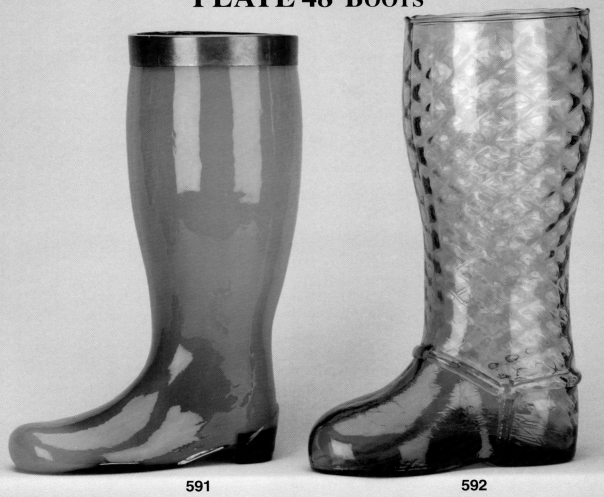

591 592

593 594

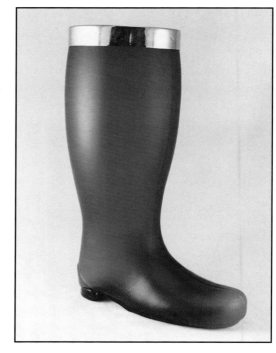

(591A) Same as (591), frosted green with a silver-colored band. 10" high, 7³/₈" long.

The bootees shown below were made by the Fenton Art Glass Company of Williamstown, West Virginia. They are the same type of shoe as those shown on Plate 55, all measuring 4¹/₄" long and 2¹/₄" high.

(728A) (728B) Emerald green and carnival OVG, both dating 1938–39.

(728C) (728D) Amber, and blue without opalescence, both dating 1938–39.

(728E) (728F) Topaz (vaseline) and rose, both dating 1938–39.

(728G) Wistaria, dating 1938–39.

PLATE 55 FENTON BOOTEES

712 **713** **714** **715** **716**

717 **718** **719** **720**

721 **722** **723** **724**

725 **726** **727** **728**

PLATE 56 Assorted Shoes

729

730

731

732

733

734

735

736

737

738

739

740

741

742

743

744

PLATE 1

The Daisy & Button shoe produced by George Duncan & Sons of Pittsburgh, Pennsylvania, was made according to the patent issued to John E. Miller on October 19, 1886. Miller's method of pressing a glass slipper left the front of the shoe open down the center. A wooden form or "last" was inserted and both sides were brought together while the glass was still pliable (Fig. 2). Both large and medium Daisy & Button shoes were made by Duncan in crystal, amber, blue, canary (vaseline) and old gold. An opalescent crystal was made in the medium size but this is scarce, as is the medium shoe in crystal with ruby-stained buttons, heel, toe and trim. In 1995, two large Duncans with ruby-stained buttons, heel, toe and trim were found in two different areas of the country. They are rare and are the only ones known. The shoes measure $5^{3}/_{4}$" x 3"

and 5" x $2^{1}/_{2}$", give or take $^{1}/_{8}$". Some are marked PAT'D OCT. 19/86 on the inside but are read from the bottom. Others are unmarked.

Many of the shoes have advertising on the sole. This was one way many firms could advertise and the same mould was used for all—only the plate was changed. A plate with the advertisement was placed in the mould before pressing the shoes. Some of the advertisements used on the large Duncan are:

J. C. BRANDT, SAINT LOUIS
CRYSTAL SLIPPER
CRYSTAL SLIPPER BOSTON THEATER
KAST'S
ROSENTHAL'S
SCHLIEK & CO.
S D SOLLERS & CO FINE SHOES
SOLLERS & Co No 18 N 8th St.

Figure 1. "Crystal Slipper" at the Boston Theater was one of the advertisements found on the large Duncan shoe. The above advertisement appeared in the Christmas 1890 *The Ladies' Home Journal* for Lablache Face Powder, with an endorsement by Marguerite Fish who portrayed Cinderella in "Crystal Slipper."

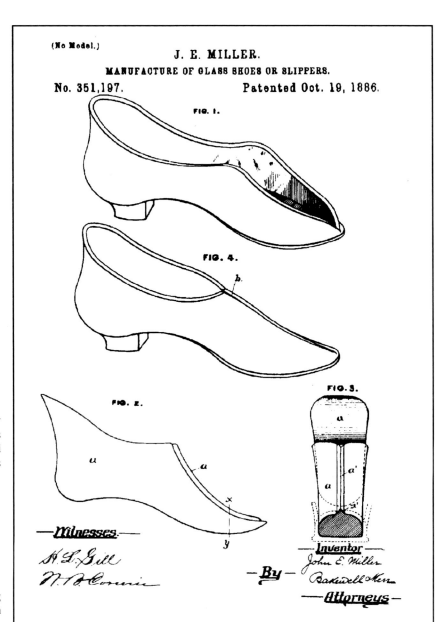

Figure 2. The John E. Miller patent used by George Duncan & Sons for creating a pressed glass slipper. Under this design, a wooden last was used to close both sides of the shoe while the glass was still pliable.

Figure 3. *(Below)* Duncan shoe with the following imprinted on sole: SOLLERS & CO. No 18 N 8th St Phila Pa.

Figure 4. This Daisy & Button shoe appeared with an assortment of novelty and pattern glass items made by the U. S. Glass Company's Factory "D" (George Duncan & Sons) after 1891. Reprinted with permission from *U. S. Glass From A to Z.*

SOLLERS & CO. NO 18 N 8th St Phila Pa (Fig. 3).

Advertisements on the medium shoes are:

J. C. BRANDT, SAINT LOUIS
BROWN & BRO
SOLLERS & CO FINE SHOES
SOLLERS & Co. No 18 N 8th St.

An advertisement in the Christmas 1890 *The Ladies' Home Journal* for Lablache Face Powder has an endorsement by Marguerite Fish who portrayed Cinderella in "Crystal Slipper" at the Boston Theater, Oct. 4, 1888 (Fig. 1). "Crystal Slipper" had been one of the advertisers appearing on the Duncan shoe.

(1) Large amber Duncan shoe has six lace holes on each side and a clear solid heel. SOLLERS & Co No 18 N 8th St. on the sole.
(1A) Same as (1) but 5³/₄" long and 3" high. This shoe is rare and only two are known.
(2) Large crystal Duncan shoe with mesh sole.
(3) Large blue Duncan shoe with mesh sole.
(4) Large canary (vaseline) Duncan shoe, PAT'D OCT. 19/86 SCHLIEK & CO on the sole. I do not know if the perfume bottle originally came with the shoe, but they were purchased together in 1972.

(5) Large old gold Duncan shoe.
(6) Crystal Diamond pattern shoe has six lace holes on each side, a clear solid heel, plain toe and a diamond mesh sole which is slightly concave. Also known in amber (740) and blue (6A). Scarce. 5³/₄" long, 2⁵/₈" high, c. 1880s.
(6A) Same as (6) and (740). Blue.
(7) Medium crystal Duncan shoe has four lace holes on each side, a clear solid heel and plain toe. J. C. BRANDT, SAINT LOUIS PAT'D OCT. 19/86 on the sole.
(7A) Same as (7) without advertisement. Old gold. 5" long, 2¹/₂" high.
(8) Medium crystal Duncan shoe with ruby-stained buttons, heel, toe and edging. Mesh sole. Scarce. Marked PAT'D OCT 19/86.
(9) Medium canary (vaseline) Duncan shoe with Daisy & Button perfume bottle whose label reads HANDKERCHIEF PERFUME PHILA. NOVELTY PERFUME CO.
(10) Medium blue Duncan shoe, PAT'D OCT. 19/86.
(10A) Same as (10). Blue frosted. 5" long, 2¹/₂" high.
(11) Medium opalescent crystal Duncan shoe Marked PAT'D OCT. 19/86. This color is scarce.
(12) Medium amber Duncan shoe. PAT'D OCT. 19/86 on the sole.

PLATE 2

(13) Crystal Finecut shoe has front opening which was closed over a last. Toe area is similar to the Smith Patent (Fig. 5) which was used by Bryce Brothers. Three lace holes on each side, mesh sole and clear solid heel. This shoe with the Smith patent toe is known in crystal, amber, blue and vaseline. 5⅞" long, 3¼" high, c. 1880s.

(14) Amber Finecut shoe is the same as (13) except the toe area shows that the front closure was made by using the Miller patent (Fig. 2) as done by George Duncan & Sons. Figure 6 compares the Smith patent toe with the Miller patent toe. Perfume bottle is Daisy & Button and label reads MARIE STUART. This shoe with the Miller patent toe is known in crystal, amber and vaseline. 5⅞" long, 3¼" high, c. 1880s.

(15) Same as (14) including the toe. Vaseline.

(16) Gold Daisy & Button open front shoe. This is another shoe which had the two sides brought together over a last but this one remains slightly open all the way to the toe which was made in the manner of the Miller patent (Fig. 2). There are no lace holes at all on this shoe. It has a mesh sole and clear solid heel. In addition to the colors shown it was also made in crystal. 5⅞" long, 3" high, c. 1880s.

(17) Same as (16). Blue.

(18) Same as (16). Amber.

(19) Same as (16). Vaseline.

(20) Opaque white (milk glass) Daisy & Button with solid heel, hollow sole and horizontally ribbed band from top to heel (Fig. 8). There are four oval "fasteners" on the vamp, the fifth and top one is rectangular. Shown in the March 1903 edition of the *Baltimore Bargain House Catalog* is a shoe containing a bottle of perfume. It seems to have the same oval fasteners as described above (Fig. 9). 4⅞" long, 2⅜" high.

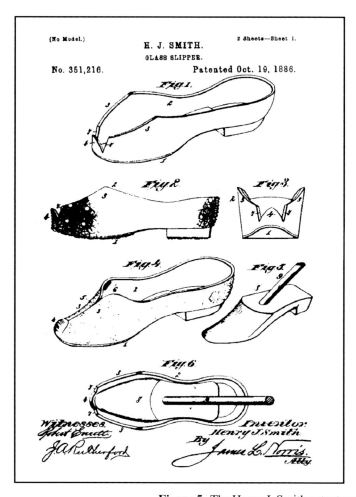

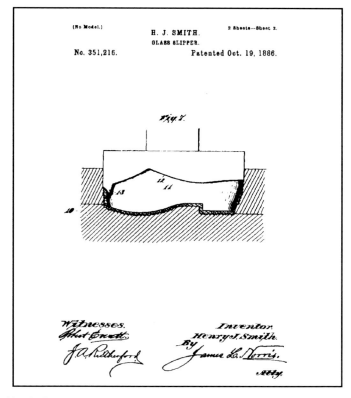

Figure 5. The Henry J. Smith patent used by the Bryce Brothers glass company.

PLATE 9

(101) Crystal Cane pattern shoe with high front has a fine mesh sole, plain toe and clear solid heel. The plain front panel has twelve lace holes on each side and the top edge dips slightly on both sides. A variation which may be found has a zig-zag line around the top edge. This shoe is known in crystal, amber, blue, aqua, gold and opaque white. Another variation on this mould has a heel which flares out at the bottom (107A). $4^5/_8$" long, $2^1/_4$" high, c. 1880s.

(102) Light blue frosted boot laced in front. The color appears to be stained. $2^3/_4$" long, $2^5/_8$" high.

(103) Same as (102). Frosted crystal. It was also made in crystal (103A).

(103A) Same as (103). Crystal.

(104) Crystal shoe which is part clear, part stippled, also made in dark amber (root beer), blue and vaseline (104A). The sole is hollow, the bow is horizontally ribbed and there are four hobnails on the right side. The top edge dips down at the back. This shoe was made in Sweden and appeared in two different catalogs, one dated 1910 (Fig. 24), the other dated 1932 (Fig. 25). They were described as ashtrays. $4^3/_4$" long, $1^3/_4$" high, c. 1900–1930s.

(104A) Same as (104). Vaseline. A scarce color for this shoe, also made in Sweden as evidenced by the 1910 and 1932 catalogs. Measures $4^3/_4$" long, $1^3/_4$" high.

(105) Same as (101). Blue.

(106) Same as (101). Gold.

(107) Same as (101). Amber.

(107A) Same as (101). Light amber Cane pattern with a differently shaped heel that flares out. The top opening on this shoe dips down on the sides but is high in front.

(108) Almost the same as (101) but this has a V front and a zig-zag line around the top. Amber.

(109) Small amber boot in Daisy & Square pattern on an oval pedestal which has a scalloped edge. The boot buttons on the left side and was made in crystal, amber, blue (109B) and vaseline (109A). Scarce. 3" long, $3^1/_8$" high, c. 1880s.

(109A) Same as (109). Vaseline.

(109B) Same as (109). Blue.

(110) Same as (109). Crystal.

(111) Same as (108). Blue.

(112) Same as (104). Root beer color.

(113) Very similar to (104), but in a Basket Weave pattern instead of stippled. It does not have any hobnails on the side and the shape of the hollow sole is slightly different. Measuring 5" long, $1^7/_8$" high.

(114) Same as (104). Blue.

	150				*7 J*					*130.*		
Knifhållare.				Cigarrkopp.				Cigarrkopp.				
N:o	mm.	v.-t	Kr.	N:o	mm.	v.-t.	Kr.	N:o	mm.	v.-t	Kr.	
1202	87	3,6	12	1203	115	4,7	12	1204	122	5	10	

Figure 24. "Pris-Courant öfver Glasvaror" glassware catalog from the FIRMA R. O. BRAUER & C:O, Transjö, Sweden. This 1910 catalog featured a crystal shoe with an assortment of ashtrays. Courtesy of the Rakow Library, Corning Museum of Glass.

Cigarr-koppar						
	Pressade			Pressade		
	N:o	Längd mm.	Pris pr 100 st. Kr.	N:o	Längd mm.	Pris pr 100 st. Kr.
	1392	115		1393	122	

Figure 25. A later glassware catalog from Transjö, Sweden, dated 1932 featured the same shoe with a different assortment of ashtrays. Courtesy of the Rakow Library, Corning Museum of Glass.

PLATE 10

(115) Crystal shoe, English. Part stippled, part plain, with a completely hollow sole and slightly indented heel. This shoe is seldom found in mint condition, often having nicks and chips on both the top edge and/or around the sole and heel. There are variations such as a vertical row of four hobnails on the right side or a scalloped top edge. This one is plain. It is known in crystal, amber, blue (115A), black (115B), teal (115C) and purple/white slag. 4¾" long, 2½" high.

(115A) Same as (115). Blue, 2⅝" high.

(115B) Same as (115). Black, 2⅝" high.

(115C) Same as (115). Teal.

(116) Opaque white shoe with a bow on the front, tiny beading around the top edge, and a scroll design on the toe and back. As far as I have been able to ascertain, this shoe was originally made in opaque white but with a round depression in the sole about the size of a quarter. Mosser Glass, Inc. of Cambridge, Ohio, has been making copies of this shoe in many colors since 1973. Although their shoe has a slightly concave sole it does not have the quarter-sized depression (Fig. 26). 4¾" long, 2⅜" high, c. 1880s.

(117) This crystal English shoe made by Sowerby has their peacock head mark inside the shoe at the heel (Fig. 21). It also has British registry mark RD 87058, the design being registered November 15, 1887. The sole and heel are completely hollow. The sides and back are ribbed vertically and the front horizontally. It has a bow with streamers and a single row of hobnails around the top. It is known in crystal, amber, blue (117A), teal, purple/white slag and black. 4⅞" long, 2⅜" high.

(117A) Same as (117). Blue. This shoe was made by Sowerby and has their peacock head mark inside at the heel. It also has the British registry mark, RD 87058. The design was registered on November 15, 1887.

(118) Same as (115) but with four vertical hobnails on right side. Red/brown slag, purchased in England. It is also known in crystal, amber (118A), blue (118B), blue opalescent (118C) and black.

(118A) Same as (118). Amber. This shoe has four vertical hobnails on the right side.

(118B) Same as (118). Blue. This shoe has four vertical hobnails on the right side.

(118C) Same as (118). Blue opalescent, which is unusual for this shoe. The opalescence can be seen clearly around the edge of the shoe.

(119) Same as (115) but with four vertical hobnails on right side and a scalloped top. It is known in amber, blue and black (119A). This shoe has also been found in black with an original pincushion (119B).

(119A) Same as (119). In addition to the four hobnails, this black shoe has a scalloped top edge.

(119B) Same as (119), but with a scalloped top edge and a pincushion, a popular feature during the Victorian era. Black. 4¾" long, 1⅜" high.

(120) Same as (115). Purple/white slag.

(121) Same as (117). Teal.

(122) Same as (115). Amber.

(123) Same as (119). Blue.

(124) Same as (117). Purple/white slag.

(125) Same as (117). Amber.

(126) Same as (117). Black.

 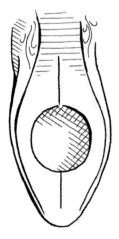

Figure 26. Comparison between the Mosser reproduction shoe (left) and the original shoe (right) with quarter-sized depression in sole (116).

PLATE 11

(127) Crystal Daisy & Button boot made by George Duncan & Sons, Pittsburgh, Pennsylvania. It has laces and lace holes on the vertical front panel. The sole is hollow, the heel solid and the top edge scalloped. The boot was made in crystal, amber, blue, canary (vaseline), old gold (127A) and crystal with ruby-stained buttons, heel, front and back panels and top edge. 4³/₄" long, 4¹/₄" high, c. 1880s.

    This boot has been copied by Degenhart, Boyd and Fenton but the original is not too difficult to identify. The front panel on the Fenton boot is plain; it has no lace holes or laces. After 1970–72 the Fenton boots were made with their logo on the bottom—"Fenton" in an oval. In the 1980s, Fenton added an "8" under the name inside the oval. In the 1990s, a "9" was added.

    All of the Boyd boots are marked ⬦Ⓑ.

    Some of the Degenhart boots are marked with a Ⓓ near the heel. The Degenhart and Boyd boots are about ¹/₄" shorter than Duncan's. Remember that Duncan boots were made only in the above mentioned colors.

(127A) Same as (127). Old gold.

(128) Crystal ribbed high shoe with scalloped edge which has a small hobnail at the top of each rib. The sole and heel are slightly hollowed and a tassel decorates the front. It is difficult to find this in perfect condition since the top edge seems to be susceptible to chipping. Made in crystal, frosted crystal, opaque light blue, opaque light green and opaque turquoise with gold trim (797). Made by Gillinder & Sons, Philadelphia (Fig. 27). 4³/₈" high, 4¹/₄" long, c. 1870s. It was advertised in an undated Gillinder catalog (Fig. 64).

(129) Same as (128). Frosted crystal. This shoe is shown in the Fall 1892 Butler Brothers Catalog and is described as "Satin Etched Shoe." The wholesale price was 74¢ a dozen (Fig. 27).

(130) Same as (127). Amber.

(131) Same as (127). Ruby-stained crystal.

(132) Same as (127). Blue.

(133) Same as (127). Canary (vaseline).

(134) Opaque light blue. Same as (128) with one small difference. The scallop at the center back is lower than the others (Fig. 28). This was a minor change in the mould.

(135) Unusual amber advertising boot on an oval pedestal. The advertisement on the side of the boot is B. HIMMELRICH & SONS BOOTS & SHOES around the outside. In the center is TRADE MARK STAR CORNER. 4¹/₄" high, 3¹/₈" long, c. 1900.

(136) Black cuffed boot with spur, probably made by Challinor, Taylor & Co. of Tarentum, Pennsylvania. It has a large "thumbprint" depression in the sole and the heel has three horizontal ridges. There is a shield outline on the vamp. Made in black and purple/white slag. 3¹/₄" high. 4" long including the spur, c. 1890.

    This boot may also be found with a solid sole which has a slightly raised chevron, the

Figure 27. Advertisement for the Gillinder shoe in the Fall 1892 Butler Brothers Catalog.

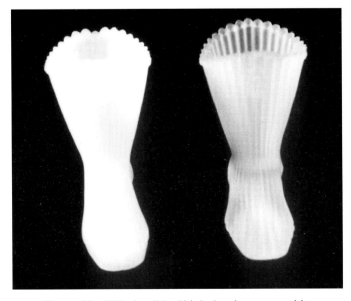

Figure 28. Gillinder ribbed high shoe in opaque white and opaque light blue (128–129) (134).

width of the sole, near the heel (Fig. 29). It can be found in black, purple/white slag and—as in (138)—a very dark purple (almost black) which may have been an unsuccessful attempt at slag. A few boots have been found with both the thumbprint depression and the chevron (136A).

The black boot appeared in a c. 1890 catalog of R. P. Wallace & Co. (probably wholesalers), 211 Wood St., & 102 & 104 Third Ave., Pittsburgh, Pennsylvania (Fig. 30).

The purple/white slag (mosaic) boot may

Figure 31. Mosaic boot seen on a catalog page from H. Leonard's Sons & Co. of Grand Rapids, Michigan (136).

NO. 3120.

be seen on a catalog page from H. Leonard's Sons & Co., Grand Rapids, Michigan. It was shown as being "filled with a bottle of fine perfume." This is the first indication that the boot was sold with a bottle of perfume or anything else (Fig. 31).

Mosser Glass, Inc. of Cambridge, Ohio, has copied the boot and makes it in many colors, some of which may be marked on the sole, near the toe, with an Ⓜ.

(136A) Same as (136), showing the thumbprint indentation on the sole and part of the chevron on the outside edges.

(137) Same as (136). Purple/white slag.

(138) Dark purple boot has solid sole with chevron (Fig. 29).

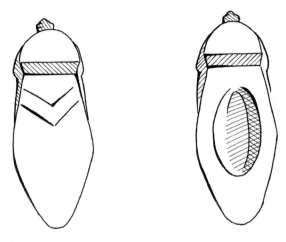

Figure 29. Challinor, Taylor & Co. cuffed boot with spur. Left, with chevron (138). Right, with thumbprint depression (136–137).

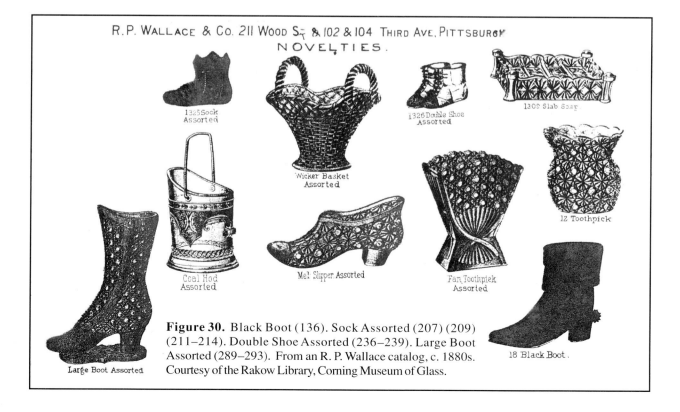

R. P. WALLACE & CO. 211 WOOD S⊤. & 102 & 104 THIRD AVE. PITTSBURGH
NOVELTIES.

1325 Sock Assorted

Wicker Basket Assorted

1326 Double Shoe Assorted

1308 Slab Soap

Coal Hod Assorted

Mel Slipper Assorted

Fan Toothpick Assorted

12 Toothpick

Large Boot Assorted

18 Black Boot.

Figure 30. Black Boot (136). Sock Assorted (207) (209) (211–214). Double Shoe Assorted (236–239). Large Boot Assorted (289–293). From an R. P. Wallace catalog, c. 1880s. Courtesy of the Rakow Library, Corning Museum of Glass.

PLATE 12

(139) Crystal, horizontally ribbed high shoe buttoned on the right. This shoe is found with buttons on either the right side or the left, so that one may have pairs. The sole is hollow, the heel is clear and solid. It has a small tassel on the front and the eight buttons curve around from the top side to the center front. It is also known in frosted crystal (140A), amber, blue, dark blue, crystal (148A), green (139A) and opaque white. 4¼" high, 4¼" long, c. 1880s.

(139A) Same as (139), green. Green is a rare color for this mould. This shoe has buttons on the right side.

(140) Same as (139) with buttons on the left side.

(140A) Same as (140). Frosted crystal. It is unusual to find shoes from this mould in frosted colors. Buttons are on the left side.

(141) Frosted crystal high shoe with a scalloped top edge. The eleven buttons on the left side have a scalloped edge. Although not apparent on this frosted shoe, there is a double row of fine stitching down the front from top to toe and down the back to the heel. There is a single row of stitching around the top edge, along the scalloped button edge and stitched buttonholes. Otherwise the shoe is plain. The sole and heel have slight depressions. Known colors are crystal, frosted crystal, blue and vaseline (798). Made by Gillinder & Sons, Philadelphia, Pennsylvania. 4¼" high, 4¼" long, c. 1870s.

   This boot had appeared in a drawing which Ruth Webb Lee credited to a Gillinder & Sons catalog in her book *Victorian Glass* (plate 206A). However, I had no confirmation that it was a Gillinder shoe until I came across the actual catalog page itself, undated and entitled "Sundries" (Fig. 64). The catalog page illustrated a shoe marked "Slipper," which appears to be a drawing of the Centennial slipper

(89–91) (89A) (94–97); a drawing of "Boot No. 1" (141–142) (151)(798); and a "Boot No. 2" (128–129) (134) (797).

(142) Same as (141). Crystal.

(143) Same as (139). Opaque white. Buttons on the right side.

(143A) Same as (143). Opaque white. Buttons on the left side.

(144) This small blue Daisy & Button boot with the delicate stippled spur is scarce and may be missing the spur. The toe and heel are clear and solid. Known colors are crystal, amber and blue. 3¾" high, 3⅝" long, c. 1880s.

(145) Same as (144). Crystal.

(146) Same as (144). Amber.

(147) Same as (139). Amber. Buttons on right.

(147A) Same as (147), frosted. Buttons on left.

(147B) Same as (147), amber. Buttons on left.

(148) Same as (139). Blue. Buttons on right.

(148A) Same as (148), in an unusual shade of blue. Buttons on the right side.

(149) Same as (139). Blue. Buttons on left.

(150) Black amethyst high shoe, probably English. Top is stippled, bottom plain. It has a small bow near the toe, is laced up the front and has a tassel at the top. The heel and sole are completely hollow. When held to the light it is a beautiful dark amethyst. It is also known in dark blue (150A). 3⅝" high, 4⅛" long, c. 1880.

(150A) Same as (150). Dark blue.

(151) Same as (141). This shoe has been found in a metal roller skate which is attached to an oval metal base. The skate was made to hold this shoe; it is a perfect fit (799)! Blue.

(152) Amber high shoe, English. The texture of the top half resembles grained leather. The bottom is plain and the sole and heel are hollow. It laces up the front and has a tassel at the top. 3⅝" high, 4¼" long, c. 1880.

PLATE 13

(153) Crystal Daisy & Button roller skate made by Central Glass Company of Wheeling, West Virginia (Fig. 34). The toe, heel and all four wheels are clear and solid. There are fifteen small lace holes on each side of the front panel. The distinctive shape with the higher front makes it easily recognizable and it has not been reproduced. Known colors are crystal, amber, blue, vaseline and lavender blue. 5¹/₂" long, 3¹/₄" high, c. 1880.

(154) Crystal roller skate in Daisy & Square pattern. Toe, heel and wheels are plain and solid. It has a fine mesh sole. 4" long, 2³/₄" high, c. 1880s. L. E. Smith made a similar skate but with a hollow sole and somewhat larger—4³/₈" long, 3¹/₈" high and it was last made in 1983. (Figs. 32 and 33).

(155) Crystal boot perfume bottle on a metal roller skate. Patented by Daniel R. Bradley on July 28, 1885. Although these bottles may still be found, they are rare on the original skate. 4³/₈" high to the top of the metal stopper (Fig. 35).

(156) This crystal roller skate bottle with six wheels is very interesting since it is marked DEPOSE on the bottom which means it was registered in France. On the left side of the ankle is the British diamond-shaped registration mark used between 1868 and 1883.

The top Roman numerals determine the class which in this case is glass (III). Beneath that is the day of the month (11). To the right of the diamond is the year (V) and the bottom letter denotes the month (G). On the left side is the parcel number (1). This design was registered in England on February 11, 1876, by James Lewis and was probably made there to be exported to France or Belgium. The DEPOSE mark would protect it from being copied in either of those countries.

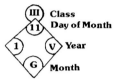

It is also possible that the item was made in France or Belgium and registered in England to keep other manufacturers on the Continent from copying the design since it would be available for sale in Europe. There is no way to be absolutely sure about the country of origin.

There are seven buttons on the right side and a pontil mark on the sole. It is 4¹/₄" high, 2⁷/₈" long.

(157) Same as (153). Vaseline.
(158) Same as (153). Lavender-blue.

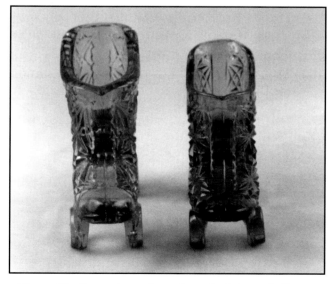

Figure 32. Comparison of two skates. Left, larger hollow sole by L. E. Smith. Right, solid sole (154) (163–166) Daisy & Square original.

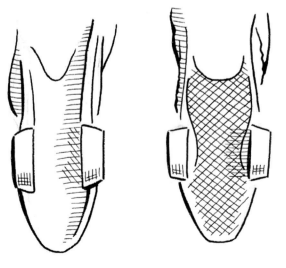

Figure 33. Soles of both skates. Left, L. E. Smith. Right, Daisy & Square original (154) (163–166).

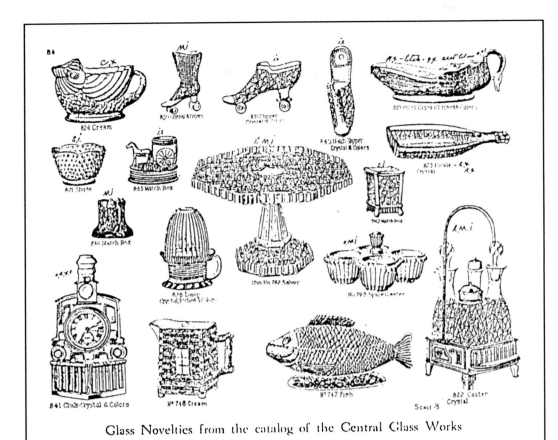

Figure 34. This catalog page of glass novelties made by Central Glass featured their crystal Daisy & Button roller skate (153) and hanging match holder (403), c. 1880.

Glass Novelties from the catalog of the Central Glass Works

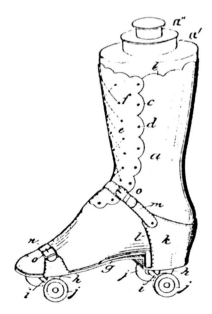

Figure 35. Drawing from the Daniel R. Bradley patent (No. 16,181) for perfume bottle on metal roller skate (155). This bottle was patented on July 28, 1885. Courtesy of the Rakow Library, Corning Museum of Glass.

(159) Same as (153). Amber.

(160) Amber roller skate in Finecut pattern has six lace holes on each side of lower front. A piece of clear glass fills in the open space above the laces. The wheels, toe and heel are plain and solid. Known colors are amber and blue. $5^{7}/_{8}$" long, $3^{3}/_{4}$" high, c. 1880s.

(161) Small blue Finecut roller skate is the same as (160) except for size and it has no laces. It is also known in crystal (161A) and amber (161B), but is scarce in any color. 4" long, 3" high, c. 1880s.

(161A) Same as (161). Crystal.

(161B) Same as (161). Amber.

(162) Same as (160). Blue.

(163) Same as (154). Aqua.

(164) Same as (154). Amber.

(165) Same as (154). Blue.

(166) Same as (154). Light amber.

PLATE 14

(167) Crystal high shoe roller skate with twelve buttons on the left side. Marked at top edge, right side, PATEИTED DEC. 1886. It is covered in a Diamond Block pattern and was designed by Herman Tappan. 4½" high, 4" long.

(168) Same high shoe as (167) but instead of a roller skate, the heel of this shoe rests on a round heelplate which reads

The "HT" in the center probably stands for Herman Tappan, the designer. The buttons are on the right side and PAT'D DEC. 1886 is at the top edge on the left side. This shoe on the heelplate has many variations. [See list after (182).] 4⅛" high, 3¾" long.

(169) Crystal high shoe roller skate. Upper portion is fine diamond mesh pattern with scalloped top edge. Shoe portion is laced in front with plain toe area and the rest is stippled alligator pattern. The heel and wheels are plain and solid. 4" high, 3½" long.

(169A) Same as (169). Blue.

(170) Opaque white high shoe roller skate appears to be the same as (169) but the insides of the wheels are flatter, leaving more space between the wheels. Between the rear wheels it reads BOTTLE MADE IN and between the front wheels, FRANCE. I have never seen a bottle which came with or would fit into this

skate. Known colors are crystal, amber (170C), opaque white (170B), green, gold, pink and lavender-blue (170A). Measures 4" high, 3¼" long.

(170A) Same as (170). Blue. Marked BOTTLE MADE IN FRANCE.

(170B) Same as (170). Opaque white. Marked BOTTLE MADE IN FRANCE.

(170C) Same as (170). Amber. Marked BOTTLE MADE IN FRANCE.

(171) Heavy crystal high shoe with four buttons on the front and trimmed in gold. The buttons are on a stippled background and there are two side panels. The top edge is indented and looks as if it might have had a cap. The rest of the shoe is plain with a solid heel. The sole and bottom of the heel have been ground. It was also made in opaque black. 4¼" high, 4⅝" long.

(172) Frosted crystal hanging match holder with side tab. The bottom of the shoe is an alligator pattern except for the clear solid heel. The upper portion is clear with a small Diamond pattern strap opposite the hanging tab. More often than not, the hanging tab is badly chipped or broken off entirely. Also known in crystal, amber and blue (172A). 3⅜" high without tab, 4" high with tab, 3⅜" long, c. 1900.

(172A) Same as (172). Blue.

(173) Crystal high shoe roller skate made by Central Glass Company of Wheeling, West Virginia (Fig. 34). Upper portion is fine diamond mesh pattern with plain top edge. Shoe is laced in front with plain toe and the remainder is a stippled alligator pattern. The heel and wheels are plain and solid. The inner sides of the wheels are flat, unlike the same model made by Degenhart and Boyd. On the latter two, the inner sides of the wheels are rounded and all

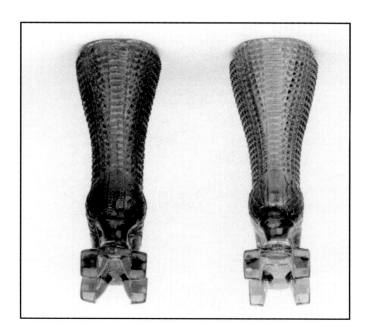

Figure 36. Left, Boyd reproduction skate (599). Right, original made by Central Glass (173) (182).

of the Boyd skates are marked (Fig. 36). Known in crystal, amber, blue (741) and vaseline (742). Two have been found advertising KAST'S on the side. 4¼" high, 3⅜" long, c. 1880.

(174) Same as (172). Crystal.

(175) Same as (167). Amber.

(176) Same as (167). Blue.

(177) Like (168) but the buttons are on the left side. On the top edge, right side, are the words PATEИTED DEC. 1886. Same heelplate. Amber.

(177A) Same as (177). Vaseline. At the present time, I am aware of only two vaseline Herman Tappan shoes with the heelplate. They both have buttons on the left side and the patent date on the top edge, right side.

(178) Like (168) but has SOLLERS & CO in place of ten of the twelve buttons on right side. PAT'D DEC. 1886 is on the top edge, left side. The heelplate is marked FINE SDS SHOES

The "SDS" is for S. D. Sollers. Blue.

(179) Same as (169). Amber.

(180) Same as (170). Green.

(181) Same as (172). Amber.

(182) Same as (173). Amber.

The known variations of shoes (167–168) and (175–178) are as follows:

The roller skate high shoe comes in crystal, amber and blue, all have buttons on the left side, all have patent date on the top edge, right side and none have advertising.

Variations of the shoe marked HT on the heelplate:

Crystal and blue, right side buttons, patent date top edge left side, no advertising.

Crystal, amber, blue and vaseline (177A), left side buttons, patent date top edge right side, no advertising.

Crystal, amber, blue and amethyst, right side buttons, no patent date, no advertising.

Variations of the shoe marked SDS on the heelplate:

Crystal, amber and blue, right side buttons (10 of the 12 buttons are replaced with SOLLERS & CO.), patent date top edge left side.

PLATE 15

(183) On March 8, 1887, George W. Bean and James Hurlbut patented their design for a Finecut "bottle holder" in the form of a high shoe (Fig. 38). The top portion is checkered and the shoe stands on a base which has a circle in the middle. The initials B&H are usually found in the circle (for the designers) but not always. The shoe was sometimes made without the initials and these are harder to find (Fig. 37). In addition, there were two moulds, one with buttons on the right and the other with buttons on the left. Therefore collectors may have pairs of these shoes. This one is a right boot in vaseline, with the initials. It was made by the Bellaire Goblet Company of Findlay, Ohio in crystal, amber, blue and vaseline. $5\frac{1}{2}$" high, $3\frac{3}{4}$" long. A reproduction of this shoe was found in August, 1988. It is crystal and has been iridized. The glass is thicker on the shoe and the base, and it has no initials. The original was not iridized.

(184) Same as (183). Vaseline. Left shoe with B&H.

(185) Same as (183). Blue. Right shoe with B&H.

(186) Same as (184). Blue. Left shoe with B&H.

(187) Same as (183). Amber. Right shoe with B&H.

    The perfume bottle standing in front of (187) is the original bottle made for these shoes. It came with (190) and is shaped perfectly to fit the shoe. The horizontal portion, just below the neck, is in the same Finecut pattern as the shoe. The bottle has a slight iridescence which the shoe does not have. It is 3" high to the top of the neck.

(188) Same as (184). Amber. Left shoe, no initials.

(189) This opaque white boot is just $\frac{1}{8}$" smaller than the others in both length and height, and has no initials on the base. The main difference is a ridge—or shelf—inside the shoe, about $\frac{1}{2}$" down from the top. It appears as if it may have held something or had a cover fit down into it. Others just like it are known in opaque white only. The maker of this boot is unknown.

(190) Same as (183). Crystal. Right shoe with B&H.

(191) Same as (184). Crystal. Left shoe with B&H.

(192) An unusual blue stippled shoe with scalloped top and a vertical row of scallops in both front and back. The shoe is partially buttoned on the right side with the upper portion unbuttoned and folded back. The heel is clear and solid and the sole is hollow. The known colors are crystal, amber, blue and vaseline (192A). 5" high, 5" long, c. 1880s.

(192A) Same as (192). Vaseline.

(193) Same as (192). Crystal.

(194) Same as (192). Amber.

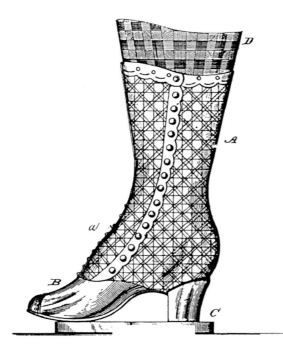

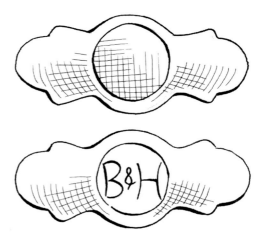

Figure 37. Base of "bottle holder" with and without the B&H (183–187) (190–191).

Figure 38. Patent drawing for B&H "bottle holder" designed by George Bean and James Hurlbut in 1887 (183–187) (190–191).

PLATE 16

(195) Crystal high shoe on round pedestal with a seven button closure on the right side. It has no decoration or etching of any kind. This boot was also made with the buttons on the left side and therefore could be collected as a pair (882) (883). They could have been intended for use as vases or drinking boots. The toe is at the edge of the base and the heel is $1\frac{1}{4}$" in from the edge. The base is 4" in diameter and the height is $7\frac{1}{8}$". Scarce, c. 1870–80.

(196) Crystal blown boot made from two pieces. It has applied leaf decorations on each side and a pontil mark on the heel. $6\frac{1}{8}$" high, $4\frac{1}{2}$" long, c. 1850–70.

(196A) Very similar to (196). Dark blue, $6\frac{3}{8}$" high and 5" long.

(196B) Another blown boot very similar to (196). Dark green, 6" high, $5\frac{1}{8}$" long.

(197) Same as (195). Has etched design around top edge and on front.

(198) Crystal German drinking boot from TUBINGEN. $5\frac{5}{8}$" high, $3\frac{3}{4}$" long, c. 1900.

(198A) Similar to (198), this boot has handpainted scenes of Kiel, Germany. The large picture at the top is marked ANDENKEN AN KIEL, KRIEGSHAFEN (souvenir of Kiel, war ships). The lower left picture shows the Marine Acad-

emy and on the right is the HOTEL SEE-BADEANSHAFT KRUPP. $6\frac{1}{2}$" high, $4\frac{3}{4}$" long.

(198B) Crystal boot with scene of town and large church. Marked ANDENKEN FREIBURG (souvenir of Freiburg). $6\frac{1}{2}$" high, $4\frac{3}{4}$" long.

(199) Blown crystal boot made from two pieces. Applied stippled straps on each side, pontil mark on heel. $4\frac{5}{8}$" high, $4\frac{5}{8}$" long, c. 1850–70. Similar boots are known in cobalt (196A) and dark green (196B).

(200) Crystal Daisy & Button boot with spur. The toe, heel and straps are amber-stained. Scarce. Also known in crystal, amber (202A) and cobalt (729). $5\frac{1}{2}$" high, $5\frac{1}{4}$" long, c. 1880s.

(201) Heavy crystal boot with metal upper portion, and three etched buttons on the right side. The top looks as if it were meant to hold something but does not appear to have had a cover. It is $1\frac{3}{4}$" deep. The bottom portion of the foot is solid and the glass is of very good quality. The sole and flat heel have been ground and are shaped as a right foot. $5\frac{1}{4}$" high, 5" long.

(202) Same as (200). Crystal, no amber stain.

(202A) Same as (202). This is the only amber boot I know of coming from this mould. Scarce. $5\frac{1}{2}$" high, $5\frac{1}{4}$" long.

PLATE 17

(203) Baby shoe is frosted crystal with gold-painted laces and bow, and painted flowers on the toe. It has a hollow sole and comes in many variations. $3^7/_8$" long, $2^3/_8$" high, c. 1920s–30s.

(204) Same as (203) in crystal, but with an unusual treatment that includes glass leaves, flowers and holders for the glass vials which themselves would hold a bit of water and flowers. The entire arrangement is embedded in what appears to be plaster of paris. The holders and flowers have also been made in colors (204A). Total height is 5".

(204A) Same as (204) but a bit more colorful. The vial holders are blue and opaque white and the glass flowers are pink.

(205) Same as (203). Frosted crystal with no decorations.

(206) Same as (204) without the added arrangement. It appears that this shoe is again being made and has been seen in quantity at flea markets.

(207) Crystal bootee, which is a favorite with collectors, has an all-over knitted pattern which continues on the bottom surface of the heel and around the edges of the hollow sole. There is a narrow ribbon around the top, just below the scalloped edge, and four horizontal ridges across the vamp. It may be found in crystal, light amber, dark amber, blue, aqua, opaque light blue and apple green (207A). It was made by King Glass Company of Pittsburgh, Pennsylvania (Fig. 15) and may be seen on a catalog page from R. P. Wallace & Co., 211 Wood St. & 102 & 104 Third Ave., Pittsburgh, Pennsylvania (Fig. 30). $3^5/_8$" long, $2^5/_8$" high, c. 1880s.

(207A) Same as (207). Apple green. Made by the King Glass Company of Pittsburgh.

(208) Same as (203). Lavender/white slag.

(209) Same as (207). Blue.

(210) Same as (205). Light blue with NEW YORK 1939 etched on the toe. Possibly sold as a souvenir of the 1939 New York World's Fair.

(211) Same as (207). Aqua.

(212) Same as (207). Dark amber.

(213) Same as (207). Opaque light blue.

(214) Same as (207). Light amber.

PLATE 18

(215) The front half of this green bootee is horizontally ribbed and has two small flowers below the opening. The rest is covered with a small Diamond pattern except for a strip of ribbing in the back. The sole is completely hollow. It comes in crystal, amber, shades of blue, vaseline and shades of green. Maker unknown. $4^1/_8$" long, $2^1/_4$" high, c. 1900.

(216) Same as (215). Green.

(217) Same as (215). Green.

(218) Same as (215). Crystal.

(219) Same as (215). Vaseline.

(220) Crystal, solid glass, Waterford bootee paperweight. "Waterford" is acid etched on the sole and there is a green and gold paper label on the top. This was purchased new in 1987. $4^1/_8$" long, $2^1/_4$" high.

(221) Same as (215). Blue.

(222) Same as (215). Blue.

(223) Same as (215). Blue.

(224) Same as (215). Teal.

(225) Same as (215). Amber.

(226) Same as (215). Blue.

PLATE 19

(227) Opaque white baby shoe with a pink bow and indented lace holes. This has the original blue and silver label of Lornita Glass which was located near Point Marion, Pennsylvania. The shoe was blown in the mould, and is very thin and glossy in appearance. The same shoe was made by Degenhart Crystal Art Glass in opaque white and custard. We do not know when Degenhart first introduced it, but the Lornita shoes are c. 1930s.

The glass appears a bit more dense on some of them so perhaps they are the later ones. Mrs. Erna Burris, who worked at Degenhart for many years and was the curator at the Degenhart Museum, remembers some of them being painted there. This only adds to the confusion of which ones were made by Lornita and which were made by Degenhart, unless the Lornita label is present. 4$\frac{1}{8}$" long, 2$\frac{1}{4}$" high.

(228) Handpainted flowers. It has the same glossiness as (227), probably made by Lornita.

(229) Color is more dense than (227) and (228).

(230) Color is more dense and painting not as well done as (227) and (228).

(231) Handpainted, same as (228) with original Lornita label. There is a name on the sole, perhaps that of the artist, that is not quite legible.

(232) Opaque white baby shoe with remains of paint has four deeply indented lace holes. 4$\frac{3}{8}$" long, 2$\frac{1}{4}$" high, c. 1900.

(233) Same mould as (232) with frosted finish and handpainted flowers and bow. This bootee may be found with different decoration (233A).

(233A) Similar to (233), this bootee is covered with bright, handpainted flowers. 4" long, 2$\frac{1}{4}$" high.

(234) A frosted crystal baby moccasin has stitching around the top and down the front, forming gathers around the vamp. Also made in crystal, both are rare. 4$\frac{3}{8}$" long, 2$\frac{3}{4}$" high.

(235) Blown iridescent bootee with pontil mark on the bottom. This bootee has been found in other iridescent colors (235A). 4$\frac{1}{8}$" long, 3$\frac{1}{8}$" high.

(235A) Same as (235), but of different iridescent colors including amethyst, green, blue and gold. Some collectors refer to this as the Tiffany bootee but I doubt that there is any connection. 4" long, 3" high.

(236) An attached pair of baby shoes in opaque blue, made by the King Glass Company of Pittsburgh, Pennsylvania, listed in their catalog as a "double shoe" (Fig. 15). It was also listed this way by R. P. Wallace & Co., Pittsburgh, in their c. 1880s catalog (Fig. 30). Made in crystal, amber, blue and opaque blue. 3$\frac{1}{8}$" long, 2" high, 2$\frac{5}{8}$" wide, c. 1880s.

(237) Same as (236). Amber.

(238) Same as (236). Crystal.

(239) Same as (236). Blue.

(240) Amber Daisy & Button bootee marked PAT'D OCT 1ℓ/86. Probably made by George Duncan & Sons using the method patented by John E. Miller (Fig. 2). Some of the Duncan bootees have the patent date on the sole while others do not. They were made in crystal (240A), amber, blue and vaseline; in 25 years I have seen and known only one in crystal. 4$\frac{1}{4}$" long, 2$\frac{3}{8}$" high. There are three different bootees known as Daisy & Button. This one by Duncan is the first. Its opening comes to a point and is somewhat wide. The second was made by Fenton and is narrower with a round toe. The third maker is unknown, and this bootee has the widest area of all, and an even rounder toe. Figure 62 demonstrates that it is easy to tell them apart by looking at the toe area from the bottom of the bootee.

(240A) Same as (240). Crystal, a rare color.

(241) Same as (240). Vaseline.

(242) Same as (240). Blue.

PLATE 20

(243) Blue boot jar with lid, on round base. It has a Finecut pattern on the underside of the lid and on the underside of the base. Either this type or (245) was advertised in the Butler Brothers Christmas Catalog of 1889 (Fig. 40) as OUR "FUNNY" INK STAND and was to retail for 10¢. While the bases are exactly the same size, this boot and its lid are smaller than (245). The difference is enough to keep the lids from being interchangeable even if the colors were the same. The height with the lid is $2^{13}/_{16}$", and the base diameter is 3". It was made in crystal, amber, blue and gold (243A). Neither of the boot jars have been reproduced, c. 1880s.

(243A) Same as (243), without the lid. Amber. The lid for (243)—with the Finecut pattern on the underside—would fit this shoe. But the snowflake lid for (245) would not. Height without a lid is $2^1/_2$".

(244) Same as (243). Crystal.

(245) This amber boot jar has the same base as (243) but its lid has an embossed snowflake design on the top and the boot and lid are larger than (243) and (244). Known colors are crystal, amber and blue. 3" high with lid and 3" base diameter. It was in the Bryce, Higbee & Co. Catalog of 1887, where it was described as UTILITY BOOT—INK with lid and UTILITY BOOT—TOOTHPICK OR MATCH SAFE without lid (Fig. 39).

(246) Same as (245). Blue.

(247) Same as (245). Crystal.

(248) Amber man's shoe with a completely hollow sole and a row of large six-sided hobnails around the sole and heel. There are four lace holes on each side and a lace in the top two. This shoe is scarce and other known colors are crystal, blue, vaseline (248A) and opaque white with handpainted flowers (248B). It has not been reproduced. $3^7/_8$" long, $2^1/_8$" high, c. 1880s.

(248A) Same as (248). Vaseline.

(248B) Same as (248). Opaque white with hand-painted flowers.

(249) Same as (248). Crystal.

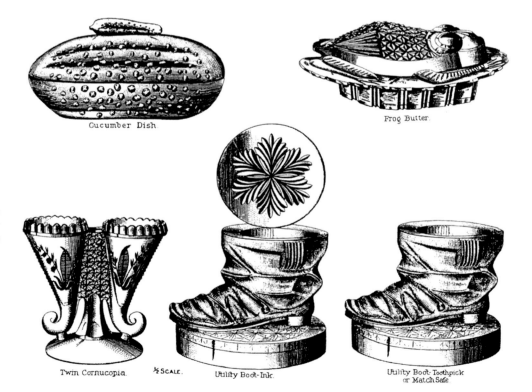

Cucumber Dish.

Frog Butter.

Figure 39. From an 1887 Bryce, Higbee & Co. catalog, this assortment of novelties included the Utility Boot Ink and Match Safe.

Twin Cornucopia.   ½ Scale.   Utility Boot-Ink.

Utility Boot-Toothpick or Match Safe.

Figure 40. The same Utility Boot Ink appeared in an advertisement in the 1889 Butler Brothers Christmas Catalog (243).

(250) Same as (248). Blue.

(251) Blue jockey boot with completely hollow sole and heel. Most of it is stippled and the heel has four horizontal ridges. It is known in crystal, dark amber, blue, black, black amethyst and black red. 3¹/₈" high, 4" long, c. 1880s. Some are marked "M. DAWSON, TRAINER, J. WATTS, JOCKEY" around the top, and in front "LORD ROSEBERY'S LADAS, WINNER OF DERBY, 1894." English.

(252) Same as (251). Dark amber.

(253) Same as (251). Crystal.

(254) Same as (251). Black amethyst.

(255) A lovely teal boot with a finely stippled background. On each side is a vine and leaf design while the front and back each have a different raised design. There are fine horizontal ridges at the ankle, the sole and heel have been ground which enables the boot to stand firmly.

This boot was made two different ways, with a solid foot or one which is hollow to the toe. It is easier to find the boot with the solid foot, which is known in teal, crystal, dark green, dark green with a silver band (257A), amber, blue (255B), smoke (255C), opaque white (255D) and opaque blue (255A). The boot with the hollow foot was made in crystal (255F) and opalescent, (255E). 4¹/₄" high, 3¹/₂" long, c. 1880s.

(255A) Same as (255). Opaque blue.

(255B) Same as (255). Blue.

(255C) Same as (255). Smoky color.

(255D) Same as (255). Opaque white.

(255E) This opalescent boot looks the same as (255) but it has a hollow foot as opposed to a solid one. 4¹/₂" high, 3³/₈" long.

(255F) Another boot similar to (255) but with a hollow foot. Crystal. 4¹/₂" high, 3³/₈" long.

(256) Same as (255). Crystal.

(257) Same as (255). Dark green.

(257A) Same as (257). Dark green with a silver band around the top.

PLATE 21

(258) Large, heavy green shoe which is shaped as a right shoe. There is a bow in front, a row of beading around the top, five scallops at the back and a turned-up toe. 6½" long, 3⅝" high, c. 1886. This shoe was shown in the wholesale Spelman Brothers Catalog for Spring 1886, listed at $2.25 for one dozen, four colors, assorted, ⅓ dozen in box. This was rather expensive since most shoes were selling for about 80¢ per dozen at that time (Fig. 41).

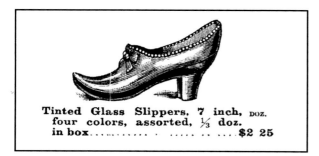

Tinted Glass Slippers, 7 inch, DOZ. four colors, assorted, ⅓ doz. in box.................................$2 25

Figure 41. Advertisement from the Spelman Brothers Special Bargain Catalog, Spring 1886 (258–261) (265). Courtesy of the Rakow Library, Corning Museum of Glass.

(259) Same as (258). Vaseline.
(260) Same as (258). Crystal.
(261) Same as (258). Blue.
(262) Plain blue shoe whose only decoration is a scalloped edge just below the top, down the front and across the toe. There are six lace holes on each side and a mesh sole. It is known in crystal and blue which are scarce, and opaque white which is rare. 6" long, 2⅝" high, c. 1890.
(263) Same as (262). Crystal.
(264) Opalescent vaseline with gold metal trim. Also comes with different metal trim on vaseline (264A). The other known colors are crystal (264B) and green (264C). Probably English. 5" long, 2¼" high, c. 1890.

(264A) Same as (264). The metal trim on this shoe is different.
(264B) Same as (264) but this shoe is crystal and the metal trim is a fancy bow on the front.
(264C) Same as (264). Dark green. The metal trim is the same as on shoe (264).
(265) Same as (258). Amber.
(266) Amethyst man's bedroom slipper. This was made in many colors and is supposed to be a pipe holder with the stem of the pipe resting where the shoe dips down in front (Fig. 42). They were probably made in the 1940s or 1950s. An amber one has been found which is marked on the sole WELLSBURG LODGE NO. 2 AF & AM 1799–1952 (269A) and also a frosted crystal one marked COMPLIMENTS OF CRESCENT GLASS CO. WELLSBURG, W. VA. (267A), 5⅛" long, 1½" high.
(267) Same as (266). Crystal.
(267A) Same as (267), frosted. The sole is marked: COMPLIMENTS OF CRESCENT GLASS CO. WELLSBURG, W. VA.
(268) Same as (266). Opaque white.
(269) Same as (266). Amber.
(269A) Same as (269) but marked with the following on the sole: WELLSBURG LODGE NO. 2 AF & AM 1799–1952.
(270) Same as (266). Frosted amber.
(271) Same as (266). Green.
(272) Same as (266). Blue.
(273) Same as (266). Ruby.

Figure 42. Man's bedroom slipper pipe holder (266–273).

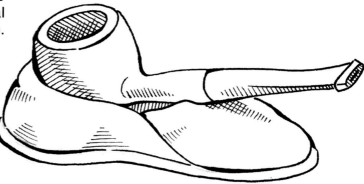

PLATE 22

(274) Very plain crystal shoe with slightly hollow sole and a solid heel. The only decorations are scallops just below the top edge. 4³/₄" long, 2⁵/₈" high, c. 1910.

(275) Crystal shoe the same as (274) but with a lower heel. The heel, scallops and center front are gold. Marked "Souvenir of Boyertown, Pa." This shoe in crystal was advertised in the Butler Brothers catalogs for 1914 and Spring 1915 at 39¢ a dozen wholesale (Fig. 43). 5" long, 2" high.

(276) Crystal lady's shoe with a small flat bow and stippled finish. It appears in the February 1918 Butler Brothers Catalog, which lists available colors as "taupe, champagne, steel blue" (Fig. 45). It was also advertised in *The Pottery, Glass & Brass Salesman* (undated) by the Lancaster Glass Company, Lancaster, Ohio (Fig. 44). They did not mention available colors but wrote "There is also a little SLIPPER that is 'too cute for anything.'" It has been found in crystal, both smooth and stippled, smooth painted grey (288), a stippled light marigold carnival (276A), amber (277A) and smooth, painted taupe (277B). Measures 4³/₈" long, 2¹/₂" high.

(276A) Same as (276). Light marigold carnival.

(277) Same as (276). Crystal, not stippled.

(277A) Same as (277). Amber.

(277B) Same as (277). Painted taupe.

(278) Same as (275). Opaque white with gold trim.

(279) Same as (278). Opaque white.

(279A) This shoe is from the same mould as (279) and although it is opaque white, it has a greyish cast to it. 5" long, 2¹/₈" high.

(279B) Same as (279). Handpainted flowers all around the shoe. A fan-shaped foil label on the sole reads RAINBOW HAND DECORATED.

(280) Opaque white shoe with embossed flower and trailing vine on each side. Has hollow sole, solid heel and front fasteners. 5" long, 2¹/₈" high.

Figure 43. Advertisement for the Lady's Slipper that appeared in Butler Brothers Catalogs from 1914 and Spring 1915 (275).

Figure 44. An undated advertisement appearing in *The Pottery, Glass & Brass Salesman.* (276–277) (288).

PLATE 23

GLASS NOVELTIES

A sho... of g... lively

...ers that are called for all the year because they ... excellent favors and souvenirs. Put in a select... suggest them to your customers.

Lady's Slipper — 4 in., fired, solid colors, taupe champagne, steel blue. 1C1006—Asstd. 1 doz. in box......Doz. **92c**

Rabbit—2½x3½, ... matt painted ... and amber, pink ... Each in box.

Figure 45. Part of an advertisement for the Lady's Slipper from a Butler Brothers Catalog, dated February 1918 (276–277) (288).

(281) Same as (280). Ruby-stained and marked "Souvenir of Windsor, N. S."

(282) Same as (275). Green, "Souvenir Williamsburg, Pa."

(283) Same as (274). Light green, gold trim and marked "Geraldine 1941."

(284) Same as (275). Ruby-stained "Souvenir Sterling, Ill."

(285) Same as (274). Ruby-stained.

(285A) Same as (285) with DAUGHTER etched on the left side. 4¾" long, 2⅝" high.

(286) Opaque blue with embossed flower and vine on each side. The only difference between this shoe and (280) appears to be differently shaped vines from the flower to the back. Trimmed in gold. Also found in crystal (286B), light amber opalescent (286C), teal and opaque white (286A). 5" long, 2⅛" high.

(286A) Same as (286). Opaque white.

(286B) Same as (286). Crystal.

(286C) Same as (286). Amber opalescent.

(287) Same as (286). Teal. Gold trim.

(288) Same as (277). Painted dark grey (Figs. 44 and 45).

(289) Amethyst high shoe. The patent for this was issued to Herman Tappan of New York City on December 14, 1886 (Fig. 47). He called the shoe a "bouquet holder" and on the fiddle-shaped base it will usually read BOUQUET HOLdER on one side and on the other side, PAT. APPLIED FOR or PATENTED DEC. 1886. This one has PAT. APPLIED FOR. There are two blue ones which, from the color and appearance of the glass, seem to be original but one reads PAT. APPLIED FOR and nothing else; the other has nothing at all on the base. There are variations but they are uncommon. Two bouquet holders have been found (amber and blue) with WOODSIDES BOOTS & SHOES on the base.

The shoe has 13 buttons on the right side and a Cane pattern covers most of it except for a stippled portion on the foot. It is 5½" high, 4⅜" long. The originals were made in crystal, amber, blue, vaseline, amethyst and apple green (289A). Amethyst is scarce and apple green is rare.

Fenton made this in 1965–66 in colonial blue, colonial amber, colonial green, orange and opaque white. The Fenton base has no lettering on it. In recent years the shoe has appeared in very dark amber and dark green and perhaps other colors as well. It has BOUQUET HOLdER on the base but the glass quality is poor and the colors are wrong. The reproductions have a more pronounced indentation at the top front than the original ones (Fig. 46).

This shoe was shown in a wholesale catalog from R. P. Wallace & Co., Pittsburgh, Pennsylvania, c. 1880s (Fig. 30).

(289A) Same as (289). Apple green. Marked BOUQUET HOLdER PAT. APPLIED FOR. Apple green is a rare color for this shoe and I know of only two in my 27 years of collecting.

(290) Same as (289). Vaseline. Marked PAT. APPLIED FOR.

(291) Same as (289). Blue. Marked PAT. APPLIED FOR. Also known in blue marked PATENTED DEC. 1886.

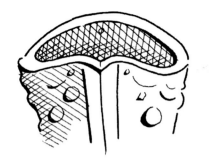 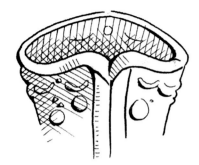

Figure 46. Left, original Tappan high shoe (289–293). Right, reproduction.

(292) Same as (289). Crystal. Marked PAT. APPLIED FOR. Also known in crystal marked PATENTED. DEC. 1886.

(293) Same as (289). Amber. PAT. APPLIED FOR.

(294) Heavy, green shoe which is plain except for a row of beading at the toe and another across the vamp and around the shoe. There is a slight depression in the sole. It may also be found in marigold carnival glass (294A). These shoes seem to have been used mainly as souvenirs. This one is a SOUVENIR OF COLUMBUS, OHIO. 4³/₈" long, 2⁷/₈" high. They were reproduced in the 1970s.

(294A) Same as (294) but this shoe is iridized a light marigold color and is sought after by carnival collectors.

(295) Same as (294). Painted orange. Marked SOUVENIR OF LORAIN, OHIO.

(296) Same as (294). Crystal. Marked SOUVENIR OF DETROIT, MICHIGAN.

(297) Same as (294). Cobalt. Marked SOUVENIR OF COLUMBIA CITY, IND.

(298) Same as (294). Opaque white. Marked SOUVENIR OF REVERE BEACH, MASS.

(299) Opalescent cranberry stirrup cup from England. Pontil mark on heel. 4⁵/₈" high, 2³/₄" long, c. 1850–1900.

    The dictionary describes a stirrup cup as "a farewell drink taken by a rider mounted to depart" or "any farewell drink." The cup did not have to be able to stand but could be placed in a pocket or handed back to the person offering it. In any event, these cups seem to have been very popular with glass blowers and were probably made as whimseys and seldom, if ever, actually used.

(300) Vaseline stirrup cup. Stands well alone. There is a pontil mark on heel. 3¹/₂ high, 3¹/₄" long, c. 1850–1900.

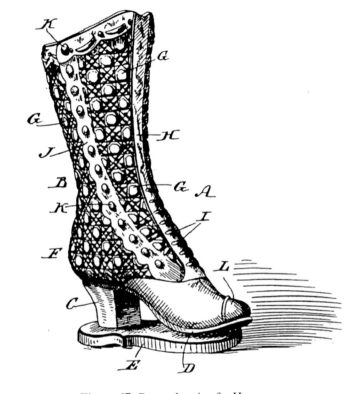

Figure 47. Patent drawing for Herman Tappan's "Bouquet Holder" (289–293).

(301) Same as (300). Amethyst. 4" high, 3¹/₄" long, c. 1850–1900.

(302) Crystal over cranberry, stirrup cup. Ground heel and sole. 5¹/₄" high, 3³/₄" long, c. 1880.

(303) Opalescent vaseline stirrup cup, purchased in England. 4" high, 2³/₄" long, c. 1880.

(304) Crystal over cranberry boot, heel applied separately. Heel, sole and top edge ground. I was told that this was purchased in a gift shop, c. 1970. 3" high, 1⁷/₈" long.

(305) Same as (304). Color is yellow-green. Purchased with (304).

(306) Same as (300). Blue, c. 1850–1900.

127

PLATE 24

(307) Frosted crystal shoe which is similar in style to the Libbey shoes (310–311) (314–315) but not the same mould. Also made in opaque white and sometimes comes with a pincushion (307B). 6³/₈" long, 3¹/₂" high.

(307A) Same as (307) with etched design on back. Similar in style to the Libbey shoes (310–311) (314–315) (310A) (311A) (311B) (311C) (929) but not from the same mould. This glass is thicker and therefore heavier. Also, the decorations used on the Libbey shoes give them a finer, more elegant appearance.

(307B) Same as (307), but more attractive than the frosted crystal. The pincushion and trim are obviously a newer addition, and the cushion was perhaps intended to replace an older, damaged one. Many older shoes did start out as pincushion holders.

(308) Crystal shoe with hollow sole and heel. Mostly covered with fine stippling, it has lacing in the front and a row of fine beading across the toe. This shoe is shown on a page from an undated catalog of Burtles, Tate & Company in Manchester, England. The page is titled PENNY LINES (Fig. 48). Also made in dark blue (308A) and black. 4⁵/₈" long, 2¹/₂" high, c. 1880s.

(308A) Same as (308). Dark blue.

(309) Crystal shoe similar to (308) with hollow sole and heel. This, too, is stippled but has a plain toe and three buttons on each side. Since this shoe is so much like (308) perhaps it, too, was made by Burtles, Tate & Company. Also made in dark blue and black. 4³/₄" long, 2¹/₄" high, c. 1880s.

(310) Crystal shoe with top edge cut in a sawtooth pattern. It has a clear solid heel and is otherwise plain. It appears to be made from the Libbey patent which was DESIGN FOR A VASE and patented March 23, 1875 (Fig. 49). 6¹/₄" long, 3¹/₂" high.

(310A) Same as (310). This shoe began as crystal, was frosted, and then cut back to clear in a very attractive design. It is rare, and the only other one like it I have seen was pictured in *Victorian Glass*, by Ruth Webb Lee.

(311) Black Libbey shoe with white enameled flowers on vamp. Opening edged in gold (Fig. 49).

Figure 48. Part of a page titled "Penny Lines" from a Burtles, Tate & Company catalog. Shows the crystal shoe with hollow sole and heel (308).

DESIGN.

W. L. LIBBEY.
Vase.

No. 8,215   Patented March 23, 1875.

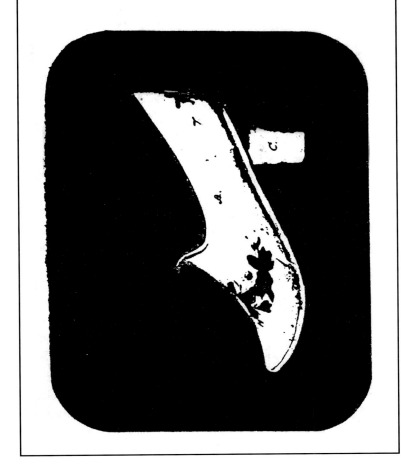

Figure 49. Libbey design for a shoe vase, patented on March 23, 1875 (310–311) (314–315).

6³/₈" long, 3¹/₂" high, c. 1875. The shoes from this mould have been found decorated in many different ways (311A) (311B) or undecorated (311C).

(311A) Same as (311). Opaque white, with hand-painted flowers above the heel and on the vamp. The heel and a thin line around the edge of the sole are painted black.

(311B) Same as (311). Opaque white and painted a deep rose on the outside. Handpainted flowers cover the front of the shoe and all around the back above the heel.

(311C) Same as (311). Opaque white, undecorated.

(312) Same as (308). Black.

(313) Same as (309) except that it has a scalloped top edge. Black. Also made in dark blue (313A).

(313A) Same as (313). Dark blue.

(314) Blue shoe with white lining has flowers on vamp which have been cut back to the white. In *Victorian Glass*, Ruth Webb Lee pictures this shoe which she says still has a paper label marked "Patented N.E.G. Co., March 23, 1875" (New England Glass Company) (Fig. 49). Also known in pink cut back to white, and beige cut back to white. 6¹/₄" long, 3¹/₄" high.

(315) Lavender shoe with gold trim and white flowers on vamp. Libbey shoe (Fig. 49). 6³/₈" long, 3¹/₂" high, c. 1875.

(316) Cased, crystal over cobalt, decorated with gold. 5⁵/₈" long, 1¹/₂" high, c. 1880–1900.

(317) Cobalt shoe bottle has three deeply indented lace holes on each side. Top of shoe, just below neck, is marked ADRIEN MAURIN. Back of the shoe above the heel is marked DEPOSE PARIS. Probably an ink bottle. 4³/₈" long, 3¹/₄" high to top of neck.

(318) Shoe is cased with a deep rose inside, then white, then a clear light green on the outside. On the vamp are leaves in the same light green and a flower. 5¹/₂" long, 2³/₈" high, c. 1880.

(319) Blue Dutch style shoe. This shoe is also known in crystal and light green (319A) 8¹/₄" long, 3" high.

(319A) Light green. Same as (319) except that it has a small knob on the back of the shoe. It has also recently turned up in crystal.

PLATE 25

(320) Opaque white boot with amber flower and leaves on vamp, and amber rigaree around the top. The opaque white boots and shoes are simply opaque white glass. 3³/₄" high, 4⁷/₈" long, c. 1880. This has also been found in a larger size, 6¹/₄" high, 6" long (320A). The rigaree and flower are amber but different than those on (320).

(320A) Same as (320) but larger, 6¹/₄" high and 6" long. This boot has an open, six-petaled flower attached to a stem that continues up to the rigaree at the top. May be one of a kind.

(321) A crystal shoe, blown in the mould, with an all-over hexagonal pattern. It has a ground pontil on the heel. 6" long, 3³/₄" high, c. 1880.

(322) Cased pink, white and green boot, the green being aventurine (a type of glass that is speckled with oxidized metallic particles). Therefore this would be described as "spangled." Without metallic flakes or streaks it is called "spatter." Most spatter and spangled boots and shoes are cased glass. The inside layer is usually white, the middle layer has the color and the outside is a layer of clear glass. There is applied crystal rigaree around the top and a crystal leaf across the vamp. All of the boots pictured on this page came from England. 3³/₄" high, 5" long, c. 1880.

(323) Cased spangled boot in dark red, orange, brown, white and green aventurine.

(324) Cased spatter boot in white, yellow and dark red colors.

(324A) Same as (324). Opaque white on the inside, pink and yellow in the middle layer, and clear glass on the outside. The rigaree around the top and the leaf across the vamp are both crystal.

(324B) Same as (324). Opaque yellow boot cased in clear glass. Crystal rigaree and vamp. 4" high, 5" long.

(325) Cased spatter boot in green and white.

(326) When the boots and shoes are cranberry there are only two layers of glass, clear over cranberry. Crystal leaf and rigaree.

(327) Cased spatter boot in white, yellow, green, blue and rust.

(327A) Same as (327). Opaque white on the inside; red, green, white and yellow in the middle layer; clear glass on the outside. Crystal rigaree and vamp.

(328) Crystal over cranberry boot with crystal flower, leaves and rigaree.

(329) Cased spatter boot in dark red, white, yellow and green. Same colors as (343).

(330) Rubina (cranberry top shading to crystal bottom) boot with crystal leaf and rigaree.

(331) Cased spatter boot in pink, brown and white.

PLATE 26

All of the shoes on this page are from England and are approximately the same size, 5³/₄" long, 3" high, c. 1890.

(332) Cased spatter shoe in dark red, white, green and yellow with crystal leaf and rigaree. Same colors as (329).

(332A) Cased spatter shoe. Same colors as (325): opaque white on the inside, green and white in the middle layer, and clear glass on the outside. Applied crystal rigaree and leaf. 5¹/₂" long, 2⁵/₈" high.

(333) Cased pink and white shoe which differs from (332) in that it is striped instead of spatter. The striped shoes are more uncommon than the spatter or spangled shoes.

(334) Cased spatter shoe in blue, green, yellow, white and dark red. Same colors as (327).

(334A) Cased spatter shoe. Opaque white on the inside; pink, white and blue in the middle layer; clear glass on the outside. Applied crystal rigaree and leaf. 5¹/₂" long, 3" high.

(334B) Cased spatter shoe. Opaque white on the inside; red, white and blue in the middle layer; clear glass on the outside. Applied crystal rigaree and leaf. 5¹/₂" long, 3" high.

(334C) Cased spatter shoe. Same colors as (324): opaque white on the inside, yellow and dark red in the middle layer, and clear glass on the outside. Applied crystal rigaree and leaf. 5¹/₂" long, 3" high.

(335) Cased spangled shoe with green aventurine. Other colors are dark red, white, brown and orange. Same colors as (323).

(336) Cased spatter shoe in yellow, blue, pink and white.

(337) Cased spatter shoe in pink, brown and white. Same colors as (331).

(338) Cased spatter shoe in aqua, brown and white.

(339) Same shape shoe in transparent glass shading from pink to green (rubina verde).

(339A) Cased shoe in crystal over cranberry. Applied crystal rigaree around top, with a flower and two leaves on the vamp. 5³/₈" long, 3¹/₄" high.

(339B) Cased shoe, crystal over solid pink. Applied crystal rigaree and leaf. 5¹/₂" long, 3" high.

(339C) Opaque white glass shoe with an amber rigaree around the top, and an amber flower and leaves on the vamp. 5¹/₄" long, 3¹/₈" high.

(340) Spatter shoe mostly green with dark red, white, and a few spots of pink and yellow. Most spatter shoes have a white interior but this one is green.

(340A) Cased spatter shoe. Aqua on the inside; blue, white, aqua, dark red and light olive in the middle layer; clear glass on the outside. Applied crystal rigaree and leaf.

(340B) Cased spatter shoe. Pink on the inside; dark red, pink, blue, yellow and white in the middle layer; and clear glass on the outside. Applied crystal rigaree and leaf.

(340C) Cased spatter shoe. Butterscotch color inside; dark red, white and beige in the middle layer; clear glass outer layer. Applied crystal rigaree and leaf. 5⁵/₈" long, 3" high.

(341) Cased striped shoe in dark red and white.

(342) Cased spatter shoe in white, pink, yellow, aqua and dark red.

(343) Cased spatter shoe in dark red, white and green. Same colors as (329).

PLATE 27

All of the shoes on this plate were made in Italy. Three have paper labels and one has a note inside that indicates it was purchased in Venice in June 1966. The latter was given to the person from whom I acquired it so I do not question the date. I have never been able to find information on how to tell the age of Venetian glass, so I will give dates of purchase if they came from a retail shop and can be assumed approximate. Otherwise I will limit myself to description.

(344) Frosted multicolored millefiore with crystal heel and rolled edge. 5$^5/_8$" long, 2$^5/_8$" high. Paper label—MURANO MADE IN ITALY. Purchased in a gift shop in 1971.

(344A) This millefiore shoe is somewhat unusual in that it has a lot of black, including the heel and the rolled edge on the front. Frosted. 5$^1/_4$" long, 2" high.

(344B) A mostly crystal shoe with just a few millefiore, quite a contrast with (344A) which has dozens of them neatly lined up in rows very close together. I have never seen another Murano shoe with so few millefiore. 6$^3/_8$" long, 2" high.

(344C) Another somewhat unusual shoe which has three rows of very large millefiore, four in each row, alternating with rows of twisted blue ribbons. The sole is white latticino. Very attractive. 5$^1/_4$" long, 1$^7/_8$" high.

(345) Two paper labels—MURANO MADE IN ITALY and AN ORIGINAL CREATION BY KB MADE IN ITALY. Purchased in a gift shop in 1983. Frosted red and blue millefiore with crystal heel and ruffled edge. Measures 6$^1/_8$" long, 2$^1/_4$" high.

(345A) Same as (345) but not frosted. Red, white and blue millefiore. 6" long, 1$^7/_8$" high.

(346) Frosted multicolored millefiore with crystal heel and ruffled edge. The toe is elongated. 6$^3/_4$" long, 2$^1/_4$" high.

(347) Red, yellow and blue millefiore with crystal heel and ruffled edge. 6$^1/_4$" long, 1$^7/_8$" high.

(348) Frosted multicolored millefiore with crystal heel and rolled edge. 6" long, 2$^1/_4$" high.

(349) Blue, white and gold millefiore with crystal heel and ruffled edge, both of which contain gold flecks. 6$^3/_8$" long, 2$^1/_4$" high.

(349A) Similar to (349) but has a rolled front and is green and yellow. this shoe has a round red and silver label which reads MURANO GLASS MADE IN ITALY. 6$^1/_8$" long, 2$^1/_4$" high.

(350) Frosted multicolored millefiore with crystal heel and ruffled edge. 6" long, 2$^1/_4$" high.

(351) Frosted red, white and blue millefiore with crystal heel and ruffled edge. Measuring 6$^1/_4$" long, 2$^1/_2$" high.

(352) Frosted multicolored millefiore with crystal heel and rolled edge. 5$^3/_8$" long, 2" high.

(353) Paper label MURANO MADE IN ITALY. A miniature red, white and blue millefiore on red ground with clear heel and ruffled edge. 2$^3/_4$" long, $^3/_4$" high. This size is scarce.

(354) Frosted red, white, blue and orange millefiore. 6" long, 2$^1/_4$" high.

(355) Multicolored millefiore with crystal heel and rolled edge, both of which contain gold flecks. 5$^1/_4$", long 2$^1/_4$" high. This shoe contains a note inside indicating it was purchased in Venice in June 1966.

(356) Rubina shoe (cranberry to clear) with applied flowers and leaves across the vamp. The rolled edge is crystal as is the heel which contains gold flecks. 6" long, 2$^1/_2$" high.

(357) Same as (356) but blue to clear. Both rolled edge and heel are crystal and contain gold flecks. 6" long, 2$^1/_2$" high.

(358) Frosted Burmese-colored shoe shading from pink to yellow with crystal ruffled edge and heel. 4$^3/_8$" high, 1$^3/_4$" high.

(359) Frosted Burmese-colored shoe shading from pink to yellow with ruffled edge in same colors. 6$^3/_8$" long, 2$^1/_2$" high.

PLATE 28

All of the shoes shown on this plate were made in Italy, circa the 20th century.

(360) This shoe contains stripes of white latticino, alternating with colors, some of which are twisted and others flat. $5^5/_8$" long, $2^3/_8$" high.

(361) Red shoe has metallic flecks of gold and silver, and streaks and threads of other colors. $5^5/_8$" long, $2^1/_2$" high.

(362) Same treatment as (361) with the main color being green. 6" long, $2^3/_4$" high.

(363) Rows of white latticino alternating with twisted blue. $5^7/_8$" long, $2^1/_2$" high.

(364) Same as (362) but smaller. Measures $5^5/_8$" long, $2^1/_4$" high.

(365) Pink latticino alternating with solid white on the ribbed sole and blue on front. Crystal ruffle and heel with gold flecks. 6" long, $1^7/_8$" high.

(366) Green and white ribbed sole and pink and yellow on front. Crystal ruffle and heel. $6^1/_8$" long, $2^1/_8$" high.

(367) Yellow latticino and light blue ribbed sole. The front is yellow and twisted pink. Ruffle and heel contain gold flecks. $6^1/_2$" long, 2" high.

(368) Light pink sole, solid colors of red and yellow on front. Crystal heel and ruffle have gold flecks. $6^1/_8$" long, 2" high.

(369) All pink latticino, crystal heel and ruffle with gold flecks. $5^1/_4$" long, $2^1/_8$" high.

(370) Pink and white latticino boot. $3^3/_4$" high, $2^5/_8$" long. The boot form is scarce.

(371) Pink and white latticino, crystal ruffle and heel. The ribbed sole is white latticino. Measures $6^3/_8$" long, 2" high.

(372) The ribbed sole is white latticino, the top is twisted colors and goldstone. Ruffle and heel have gold flecks. $5^1/_4$" long, $1^3/_4$" high.

(373) Frosted shoe with white latticino and twisted colors with goldstone. Elongated toe. $6^1/_8$" long, $1^3/_4$" high.

(374) Paper label GENUINE VENETIAN GLASS FROM MURANO. MADE IN ITALY. A DECORA IMPORT. Red shoe with metallic flecks of gold and silver and streaks and threads of other colors. $5^1/_2$" long, $2^1/_4$" high.

(375) Purchased in Venice in 1969. Light blue and white latticino. Crystal heel and ruffle with gold flecks. $5^1/_8$" long $1^7/_8$" high.

(376) Sole is white and crystal, the front is cobalt and crystal. Gold flecks on crystal heel. $4^5/_8$" long, $1^5/_8$" high.

(377) Cobalt and white. In addition to the gold-flecked heel and ruffle there is an unusual decoration. On the vamp is one millefiore set in a gold flecked crystal ornament. $3^7/_8$" long, $1^1/_2$" high.

PLATE 29

(378) Baccarat-marked crystal shoe, which was made from 1956 to the mid-1970s, was designed and produced as a candy dish. In the folklore of the French province of Alsace, shoes are left on the hearth for St. Nicholas who arrives on the eve of December 6 and leaves bonbons in the shoes of the good children. This accounts for the style of this candy dish which was sold by several fine French candy makers.

The shoe is both large and heavy, measuring 10" long, 3½" high and weighs two pounds 13 ounces. A medallion design, measuring 1½", is on the back and the front is covered with horizontal grooves. The sole edge is scalloped, starting at the toe and continuing back to the heel, each scallop a bit longer than the previous one.

(379) This crystal shoe was purchased in England and I know of only one other like it. On the vamp is one large flower and there are five horizontal ridges down to the toe. The bow has four horizontal ridges and the streamers are narrowly ribbed. The large ridges start again behind the streamers and continue back to the heel on the underside of the shoe. The sole is hollow almost back to the bow and the heel is slightly indented on the bottom and about half hollow on the inside. 7" long, 3½" high, c. 1880s.

(380) A very heavy crystal shoe with a bow and four buttons on the vamp. It weighs two pounds three ounces and is solid glass except for an opening from the top down to the heel. One has been found with a black and white label marked PUKEBERG, SWEDEN. 6¼" long, 4¾" high.

(381) Although the Heisey Company never referred to this as a shoe, it is in the shape of an elf's shoe and is collected as such by shoe collectors. The correct Heisey name is #1555 Cornucopia Floral Bowl and was made in crystal from 1942 to 1956. 10" long, 3" high and weighs two pounds.

(382) Crystal shoe with stippled bow and streamers. It has a large all-over Diamond pattern with a plain toe and heel. A diamond mesh covers the front half of the sole. It was also made in amber (382A) and cobalt (382B), both of which are marked REGISTERED 64088, which means the design was registered in England in 1886. 8⅛" long, 3⅝" high and weighs one pound seven ounces, c. 1880s.

(382A) Same as (382) except that the sole is completely covered with a diamond mesh pattern from the tip of the toe to the heel. Amber, a scarce color. 8" long, 4" high.

(382B) Same as (382A). Cobalt, a scarce color.

(383) Large heavy crystal shoe from England. It is Daisy & Button and has a scalloped top edge. The bow, streamers, heel and toe are plain but the sole and the bottom of the heel have a diamond mesh pattern which shows through the plain toe. Inside, in embossed letters, it is marked THE SULTANA. 8⅜" long, 3⅞" high and weighs one pound 12½ ounces, c. 1880s.

(384) A plain crystal shoe with only a small star-shaped design on the vamp. 9" long, 2¼" high.

(385) Crystal Dutch shoe with three horizontal ridges on the vamp and three buttons on the right side. This shoe is shaped for a right foot, and was also made in iridized crystal with fine raised lines on the surface (385A). 7" long, 3⅛" high.

(385A) Iridized crystal. Same as (385) but the surface is covered with fine raised lines.

PLATE 30

(386) Large crystal shoe with a small Diamond pattern covering the back half of the shoe, all of the sole and the bottom of the heel. The front of the shoe is plain and the pattern, which is visible, is on the sole. There is vertical ribbing around the top edge. The known colors are crystal, amber, blue and opaque white. 7½" long, 3½" high.

(387) Same as (386). Opaque white with pansies painted on the vamp.

(388) Crystal Sowerby shoe has three sunbursts on each side and a row of hobnails around the top. The sole is hollow and the bottom of the heel is indented about ¼". Sowerby's embossed peacock head mark is on the inside. It is known in crystal, amber (388B), cobalt, teal (388A) and purple/white slag (388C). 7½" long, 3½" high, c. 1885.

(388A) Same as (388), teal. This shoe also has Sowerby's embossed peacock head mark on the inside.

(388B) Same as (388), amber.

(388C) Same as (388), made in purple/white slag.

(389) Crystal shoe with arches around the back half is very much like (386) in overall shape but the pattern on the sole is only on the indented portion and does not extend to the heel. The front of the shoe is plain. This shoe is shown in a catalog dated 1914 from Josef Inwald A. G., Vienna, and described as a bonbonniere (Fig. 50). Perhaps (386) is also Austrian. This shoe is known in crystal, amber and vaseline (389A). 7⅝" long, 3⅛" high.

(389A) Same as (389). Vaseline. The pattern in the front portion of the sole may be seen through the top of the shoe.

(390) Same as (386). Amber.

(391) Same as (386). Blue.

(392) Same as (388). Cobalt.

(393) Same as (389). Amber.

Bonbonniere

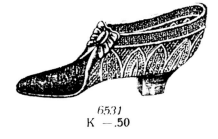

6531
K — .50

Figure 50. Shoe with arches pattern (389) (393) advertised in this 1914 catalog from Josef Inwald A. G., Vienna. Courtesy of the Rakow Library, Corning Museum of Glass.

135

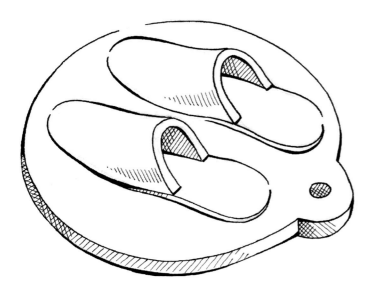

PLATE 31

(394) A round, flat, crystal match holder with a Cube pattern on the back side. The front has two slippers which are the match holders. Between them is fine horizontal ribbing for the striker. The slippers are stippled and have bows and plain toes (Fig. 51). It was also made in blue (394A). In *Victorian Glass*, Ruth Webb Lee mentions amber and opaque white but I cannot confirm these two colors. It is 4¹/₂" in diameter, c. 1880s.

(394A) Same as (394). Blue.

(395) Green boot match holder was made by Bryce, Higbee & Company, Pittsburgh, Pennsylvania., c. 1880s. They named it a "Tramp Match Safe" (Fig. 53). It also appeared in the Butler Brothers, Christmas Catalog of 1889.

The boot match holder has been made a number of different times in more recent years, since it was first manufactured in the 1880s. Each time there have been changes in the mould which are most apparent in the pattern on the back of the boot. Because these differences are difficult to illustrate, collectors should examine the backs closely for such differences. The oldest ones are probably those which have the smallest portion of solid glass in the foot and a clear sharp row of stitching near the bottom front of the shoe (Fig. 52). 4¹/₂" long.

Some of the copies have been done quite well while others are poorly done. The latest arrivals have a small rectangular gold label (if it is still attached) which reads MADE IN TAIWAN, and they have been seen in flea markets and souvenir shops.

(396) Dark blue match holder. Probably a somewhat later copy.

(397) Aqua boot. Original.

(398) Blue hanging match holder made by King Glass Company and marked PAT'D JUNE 13th 76, shown with other miscellaneous items on a catalog page. (Fig. 15). The shoe is

Figure 51. Round match holder with two slippers. There is a horizontal ribbing between them for striking (394).

Figure 52. The Tramp Match Safe. Left, probably a reproduction, since the solid glass portion is larger (396) (399–400). Right, probably the original (395) (397) (401–402).

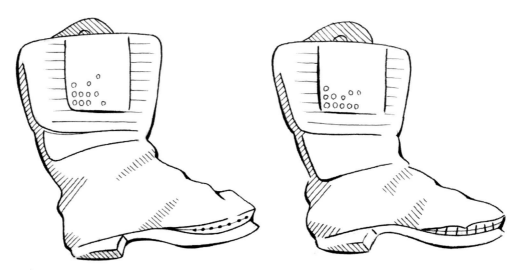

Acme Mug No.1 & 2

Acme Mug No.3

A B C Plate

½ Gal. Owl Pitcher.

Tramp Match Safe.

Over

BRYCE, HIGBEE & CO. PITTSBURGH. PA.

Figure 53. This 1889 Bryce, Higbee & Co. catalog featured the
green boot match holder (395), which they called Tramp Match Safe.

covered in a Diamond pattern and has a short
stippled ribbon on each side of a round ornament. The sole and heel are covered in a diamond mesh and the patent date is on a clear
strip under the heel. This was made in crystal
(398B), amber (398A) and blue. 6⅞" long.

(398A) Same as (398). Amber.
(398B) Same as (398). Crystal.
(399) Medium blue boot. Probably later copy.
(400) Amber boot. Probably later copy.
(401) Crystal boot. Original.
(402) Amethyst boot. Original.
(403) Amber hanging match holder made by Central

Glass Company of Wheeling, West Virginia
and shown on their novelty catalog page, c.
1880 (Fig. 34). Daisy & Button pattern with a
stippled panel from the scalloped top to the
clear toe. The flat heel has two rows of beading around it and a hole in the center for hanging. The sole is mesh. Known colors are
crystal, amber, blue, vaseline and gold. 6¼"
long, c. 1870–85.

(404) Same as (403). Crystal.
(405) Same as (403). Vaseline.
(406) Same as (403). Blue.
(407) Same as (403). Gold.

PLATE 32

Although long attributed to Bryce Brothers without confirmation, we finally know that these 11¾" celery dishes in the form of shoes were actually made by Hobbs, Brockunier & Co. of Wheeling, West Virginia. The *Crockery & Glass Journal* for October 9, 1884, page 16, stated that Hobbs, Brockunier & Co. is now producing Daisy & Button "celery dishes, mostly in the shape of a shoe" in all colors. On November 20, 1884, page 12 the journal reported: "The celery dishes are recumbent instead of upright as formerly, and are generally made in the shape of boats, yachts, shoes and other articles."

(408) Giant-size apple green Daisy & Button shoe. The pattern covers the sides, the bottom of the heel and all of the sole. Known colors are crystal, amber (408A), blue, vaseline and apple green. 11¾" long, 2½" high, 4½" wide, c. 1880s.

(408A) Same as (408). Amber.

(409) Same as (408). Crystal.

(410) Same as (408). Blue.

(411) Same as (408). Vaseline.

(412) Giant-size apple green Daisy & Button shoe. The dimensions are the same as (408) but this one has plain sides, except for four rows of stitching and a button on each side. Known colors are blue, gold (412A) and apple green, c. 1880s.

(412A) Same as (412). Gold. The plain sides of this celery dish shoe make it different from (408A).

Figure 54. Advertisement from an 1889 Butler Brothers Catalog, showing the Daisy & Button shoe holding a perfume bottle (420) with an assortment of colognes.

PLATE 33

(413) The elusive and expensive shoe lamp in crystal. Marked PAT'D JUNE 30 1868 and made by Atterbury & Company of Pittsburgh, Pennsylvania. Known colors are crystal, amber, blue (413A), light olive green (413B) and opaque white. 6" long from toe to end of handle, 3" high to top of collar.

(413A) Same as (413). Blue.

(413B) Same as (413). Olive green.

(414) Same as (413). Amber. 5¾" long, 3" high.

(415) Frosted crystal Gillinder shoe in original holder. The shoe is marked GILLINDER & SONS CENTENNIAL EXHIBITION. Gillinder & Sons of Philadelphia set up an exhibition glass factory at the Centennial site in Fairmount Park in Philadelphia. Among the many items made and sold there were these shoes, most of which were probably sold without the holder. While the shoes may still be found occasionally, the holders are scarce. The shoe is 5½" long, 2⅝" high. The holder is 7½" high.

(416) This shoe on the round base is rare. The pattern on the shoe is stippled and looks like alligator. The base is hollow and has a spray of small flowers and leaves on each side of the shoe. The shoe itself measures 3⅜" long, 2¼" high. The diameter of the base is 3⅝" and the overall height of base and shoe is 3⅜". It is known only in crystal, c. 1880s.

138

PERFUMERIES.

A Department Worthy the Attention of any Merchant--A Line of Goods which Lend Tone to the Store where they are Shown, and in the Higher Grades Lay a Foundation for a Sure Future on Sales.

Popular Prices Provide Pleasant Perfumes.

	Gross.	Doz.
......Our **Beauty Box of Phial Perfumery**—*A 5 cent gem.* Consisting of a handsome show case, show box, with picture inside and the bottles arranged on card about picture; 2 doz. vials in box. Sold only by box. *Price 3c. per bottle, or*		36
......Our **"5-Cent Slipper Bottle"**—An article universally offered as a 10-cent article, which at 5 cents makes a quick seller. 1 dozen in a box	$4 90	43
....Our **Leg Bottle Cologne for a "5-Cent Price"**—This is another of our 5-cent surprises, as it has been sold at 10 cents by the trade generally, and at that price is not high. We offer it put up 1 dozen in box, at	4 90	43
.....Our **5-Cent Baby Bottle Perfume**—*Shipped at buyer's risk in cold weather*—One of the best of sellers. Worth double the price for the novelty of the thing. Question: How could the baby be put into the bottle? Put up 2 dozen in a box	5 00	44
.....**Mirror Bottle Perfume**—*The old reliable 10-cent favorite.* This is not the common goods so generally offered. 1 dozen in box	8 00	70
.....**Our Imported Venetian Jug Vase Perfumery**—*A 10-cent crazy seller*—This item is worth more than its price for the vase alone. It is a special importation, and will not last all the season. 1 dozen in box, assorted	10 25	87
.....**Our 10-Cent Fairy Glass Slipper**—A beautiful colored glass slipper, containing a basket-pattern bottle. The chief of dime beauties. 1 dozen in box	9 25	80
......**Hoyt's Dime Cologne**—This article is too well-known by our patrons to need either description or illustration. It is the best cologne made. 1 dozen in box	8 25	72
.....**Our Heliotrope Dime Sprinkler Top Bottle**—*The very best of all 10-cent offerings.* This beautifully shaped bottle has a nickel-plated sprinkler top, and contains a genuine "way up" quality of handkerchief perfume. A popular size, and the only 10-cent sprinkler-top in America. Put up 1 dozen in fancy "Step" box	10 25	86
......**Our Wire Easel Cologne**—Consisting of 12 bottles of a high grade Cologne, put up on a Wire Easel, in spaces for same. It makes a splendid article to place on top of the show case, and sells out rapidly at "10 cents" each. An Easel with each dozen	9 75	82

Figure 55. Cologne bottles from the Butler Brothers *Cold Weather Edition "Our Drummer" Catalog* circa 1888. Pictured here are Leg Bottle Colognes (419) (420). The 5-Cent Slipper Bottle (559) is also shown.

(417) Frosted Gillinder, same as (415), but in an even more unique base which is held up by three cherubs. The base was made to fit the shoe exactly. I have never seen or heard of another like it. The base alone is 5¹⁄₈" long, 1¹⁄₄" high.

(418) Opalescent crystal shoe with British registry RD 65455. The design was registered by Burtles, Tate & Company of Manchester, England on January 15, 1887.

It has a deeply hollow sole which extends halfway up the vamp, laces in front and a bow with ribbed streamers reaching the sole. The top edge is scalloped, the heel solid, and the toe is squared. It was also made in opalescent blue (418A). 4³⁄₄" long, 2¹⁄₈" high.

(418A) Same as (418). Blue opalescent.

(419) Inkwell purchased in England. The holder is metal and the two frosted crystal shoes contained the ink. Each shoe has two small round knobs, one on the sole and one on the heel, which fit into holes of the same size in the holder. When the vertical metal knob is pushed back it raises the covers on the shoes. The

shoes themselves are narrow and somewhat similar to the Gillinder shoe. The oval-shaped inkwells are raised above the sides of the shoes (see 420) and are 2" long, 1¹⁄₈" deep. The metal holder is marked PAT. AP'D FOR and is 9" x 6⁷⁄₈" and is 5¹⁄₈" high, c. 1880s.

(420) Opaque white shoe is the same as the two shoes in the inkwell (419). The two knobs on the bottom have been ground off (the outline of one still shows) so that the shoe will stand alone. 5" long, 2¹⁄₈" high, c. 1880s.

The cologne bottles on the bottom row are each a bit different in size or shape. Some were acquired with a shoe while others were bought separately when recognized that they were the bottles which often came with shoes. All are Daisy & Button around the bottle and on the horizontal upper surface and some are iridescent. Shoes containing bottles of cologne were advertised in Butler Brothers catalogs of 1888 (Fig. 55) and 1889 (Fig. 54). The shoe in the 1889 catalog is described as 4" x 6" and appears to be in the Daisy & Button pattern.

PLATE 34

(421) Crystal triple boot match holder is stippled on the foot of the boot while a Finecut pattern covers the rest. Each boot has a tassel at the top and a row of buttons slightly to the left of center. They stand on a triangular base, which is stippled on the underside, and were made in crystal, amber (421A), blue and black by the Bellaire Goblet Company of Findlay, Ohio. Scarce. 4¹/₂" high, 4³/₈" wide, c. 1880s.

(421A) Same as (421). Dark amber.

(422) Scarce two-piece opaque white shoe (Fig. 56). It has an embossed bow on the removable front piece and swirls, scrolls and a diamond design on the sides. It is a shoe which all collectors hope to add to their collections and has not been reproduced. The maker is unknown. 7⁷/₈" long, 4⁷/₈" high, c. 1880s.

(423) New shoe (1986) made in England. Label reads GEORGIAN CRYSTAL TUTBURY LTD. 6¹/₂" long, 3" high.

(424) Crystal shoe with a mustard jar and salt and pepper shakers with glass tops. It was purchased new about 1963 and has a paper label reading MADE IN WEST GERMANY. It has been reported that the same set was made with metal tops and not as sharply cut as this one. It, too, was purchased new and made in West Germany. 5³/₈" long, 2⁵/₈" high without the shakers.

(424A) Similar to (424) but larger and not cut as sharply. There is a small, round gold label marked MADE IN WEST GERMANY. 5³/₄" long, 2³/₄" high.

(425) Crystal high-heeled shoe, plain with only an applied glass medallion for decoration. Bottom of heel and sole have been ground. Same as (429), but larger. This shoe is rare. 7¹/₈" long, 3³/₄" high.

(426) The cat in the man's shoe was made in England by Sowerby & Company and has their peacock head mark. It is completely hollow except for the cat's head. The detail is excellent, showing the leather of the shoe and the cat's fur. It has round hobnails on the sole edge and rectangular ones on the heel. 4⁷/₈" long, 3¹/₈" high, c. 1870s.

(427) Small crystal Dutch style shoe. Measures 4" long, 1⁷/₈" high.

(428) Plain crystal frosted shoe with solid heel. 5" long, 2³/₈" high.

(429) Crystal shoe with applied medallion on front. Same as (425) but smaller and with a lower heel. 4³/₄" long, 2¹/₄" high.

(430) Crystal frosted Dutch style shoe, hollow in front, back has indentation, probably for a cigarette. 4⁷/₈" long, 2" high.

(431) Same as (430). Crystal.

(432) Same as (430). Gold painted decoration.

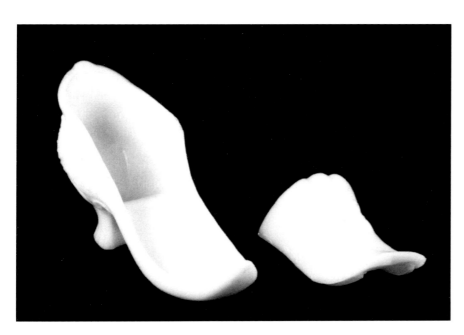

Figure 56. Two-piece opaque white shoe (422), scarce. The front piece has an embossed bow, and the sides are designed with swirls, scrolls and a diamond pattern.

140

PLATE 35

All boots on this plate have pontil marks on the heels and were most likely made in England, c. 19th century. See Plate 23, page 127 for discussion of stirrup cups.

(433) Nailsea-type flat boot flask. White loopings on crystal. Most shoe collectors desire these flasks and wish they had many more than they already own. 10½" high, 4½" wide.

(434) Small Nailsea-type flat boot flask. This size is harder to find than the large ones. Measures 5¼" high, 3" wide.

(435) Flat boot flask with white loopings on crystal. 9½" high, 4½" wide.

(436) Plain crystal stirrup cup blown in one piece, 4¾" high.

(437) Swirled crystal stirrup cup with the foot added on. A narrow strip with horizontal ribbing is applied to the back from the top to the heel. Measures 5" high.

(438) Plain crystal stirrup cup with foot added on, 4¾" high.

(439) Plain crystal stirrup cup with foot added on, 3¾" high.

(440) Crystal stirrup cup with foot added on. It has bands of cut designs and, on the bottom of the round heel, there is a rayed design which, along with a ground sole, allows it to stand securely. Like (437) this has a narrow ribbed strip applied to the back, 3⅞" high.

(441) Plain crystal stirrup cup with foot added on, 3¾" high.

(442) Plain crystal stirrup cup with foot added on. Applied glass "straps" on each side and applied strip on back, 3¼" high.

PLATE 36

Numbers (443) through (450) each have a pontil mark on the heel and were probably made c. 19th century. For information about stirrup cups, see Plate 23, page 127.

(443) Amethyst flat boot flask with opalescent spirals, 8" high.

(444) Crystal stirrup cup. The foot portion has five toes! 6¼" high.

(445) Crystal flat boot flask with five toes. Each side has a different design of etched leaves, measuring 8" high.

(446) Plain crystal stirrup cup, 4½" high.

(447) Plain crystal stirrup cup with foot added on. The upper portion is straighter than most and resembles an actual boot, 3⅞" high.

(448) Plain crystal stirrup cup with foot added on, 3⅜" high.

(449) Plain crystal stirrup cup with a thinner-than-usual foot portion, the toe of which turns up slightly, 4" high.

(450) Crystal boot with a small attached heel, measuring 3½" high.

(451) Lovely Victorian blown crystal shoe with crystal threading and applied rigaree around the top. The heel and sole are ground. 3⅝" long, 1¾" high.

(452) Same as (451). Crystal with cranberry threading. 5⅛" long, 3" high.

(453) Same as (451). Crystal with blue threading. 3⅝" long, 1¾" high.

PLATE 37

(454) Crystal high shoe bottle is laced in front and has eight buttons on the right side. 5³/₈" high, 3³/₄" long.

(455) Aqua high shoe bottle with eight buttons on the right side. GEO. S. COLBURN WEST GARDNER MASS is embossed at the top of the left side of the shoe. 5" high, 4" long.

(456) Plain crystal boot bottle has a small "5" on the sole. 4⁷/₈" high, 3¹/₂" long.

(457) Same as (456). Green. Small "10" on sole.

(458) Aqua high shoe bottle has eight buttons on the right side. On one side of the buttons is SARATOGA, on the other side is DRESSING. This bottle can also be found in dark amber (458A). 4¹/₂" high, 3⁵/₈" long.

(458A) Same as (458). Dark amber, a rare color for this shoe bottle.

(459) Crystal high shoe bottle with nine buttons on the right side. 4³/₈" high, 3¹/₂" long.

(460) Crystal boot bottle has laced front and wrinkles on the vamp and ankle. Measures 4¹/₈" high, 2⁷/₈" long.

(461) Crystal high shoe bottle has laced front, eight buttons on the right side and scallops around the top edge. 3³/₄" high, 2⁷/₈" long, c. 1880s.

(462) Crystal shoe bottle. Although very similar to (461) with the laced front, it has no buttons on the side and has a bow above the laces and scallops across the toe in addition to around the top. Both bottles probably held cologne. Marked on the sole. 4" high, 2⁷/₈" long, c. 1880s.

(463) Crystal high shoe bottle has original label around the neck and decal of a woman on the front. This bottle and/or (461) and (462) could be the ones shown in a c. 1888 Butler Brothers Catalog and described as "Our Leg Bottle Cologne." They were 5¢ each or 43¢ a dozen wholesale (Fig. 55). 3¹/₄" high, 2³/₈" long.

(464) Opaque white boot with threaded top and screw-on metal cap. I was told that these were made by Hazel Atlas Co. but I have been unable to confirm this. 2³/₄" high 2¹/₄" long, without the metal cap.

(465) Same as (464).

(466) Crystal man's overshoe advertising WALES GOODYEAR on each side. It has a tightly fitting hinged metal lid which is marked BEAR BRAND and shows a bear between the two words. It is obviously a container but the original contents are unknown. Although it is shown in a candy container book, I do not think it held candy. It is rare to find it with the lid attached and scarce even without the lid. 4" long, 2⁵/₈" high.

(467) Crystal bootee bottle has ribbing around the top below the neck. The toe is plain, the vamp stippled and the rest is Daisy & Button. There are laces and three lace holes on each side and a "T" on the bottom. 3" long, 3" high, c.1880s.

(468) Crystal bootee bottle is plain with laces and three lace holes on each side. The sole is ribbed and marked with a "V". It has four rings around the top below the neck. 2¹/₄" long, 2¹/₄" high, c. 1880s.

(469) Crystal bootee bottle is a larger version of (468). The sole is smooth but has a "V" mark. The original label, YLANG YLANG, is on the neck and in very good condition. Ylang Ylang is an East Indian tree of the custard-apple family with fragrant greenish yellow flowers. The oil obtained from these flowers is used in perfumes. 3" long, 2⁷/₈" high, c. 1880s.

(470) Plain crystal boot with wide cuff has no other decoration. Part of the original label remains on the neck. Like (468) and (469) it is ringed below the neck. 2" long, 2⁷/₈" high, c. 1880s.

PLATE 38

Numbers (471) through (476) are probably ink bottles.

(471) Crystal man's shoe bottle with laces, stitching and a threaded top. 4$\frac{1}{8}$" long, 2$\frac{7}{8}$" high.

(471A) Similar to (471) but does not have a threaded top. It does have laces and stitching and an old decal on the toe. 4$\frac{1}{8}$" long, 3$\frac{1}{2}$" high.

(472) Crystal man's shoe bottle with laces. 4$\frac{1}{8}$" long, 3$\frac{3}{8}$" high.

(472A) Plain crystal shoe with five buttons on the right side. 4$\frac{1}{8}$" long, 2$\frac{1}{2}$" high.

(473) Green man's shoe bottle with laces, horizontal ridges on each side and the remains of an old label around the neck. 3$\frac{1}{2}$" long, 2$\frac{1}{2}$" high.

(473A) Same as (473). Crystal.

(473B) Another green man's shoe bottle with horizontal ridges on each side and a raised ridge across the toe. 4" long, 3" high.

(473C) Crystal shoe bottle without laces. It has a stitching pattern on the front and horizontal ridges on each side. 4$\frac{3}{8}$" long, 3$\frac{1}{2}$" high.

(474) Crystal man's shoe bottle with laces. 3$\frac{3}{8}$" long, 3" high.

(474A) Aqua shoe bottle with five buttons on a scalloped edge on the right side. On the front of the shoe, in script, is the name EHRLICH'S. 4$\frac{1}{2}$" long, 4$\frac{1}{8}$" high.

(474B) Same as (474A). Amber.

(475) Green man's shoe bottle which has a buckle on the front, four buttons on the right side and a square toe. 4$\frac{3}{4}$" long, 3" high.

(475A) This light green shoe bottle resembles (475) in that both have buckles on the front and are green. This one has a metal ring around the neck opening. 4$\frac{3}{8}$" long, 2$\frac{5}{8}$" high.

(476) Green man's shoe bottle with ten buttons on each side of center front. 4" long, 1$\frac{7}{8}$" high.

(476A) Same as (476). Crystal. 4" long, 2" high.

(477) Opaque light blue boot most of which is covered in a leaf pattern with a plain band around the top. It has a small round indentation in the sole about $\frac{1}{2}$" in diameter. Also known in opaque white (477A). 3$\frac{1}{8}$" high, 2$\frac{3}{4}$" long, c. 1880s.

(477A) Same as (477). Opaque white.

(478) Christmas candy boot with a Santa Claus sticker has the original sealed cardboard top which reads: SANTA CLAUS'S BOOT—CHUCK FULL OF DELICIOUS CANDY PELLETS. INGREDIENTS: SUGAR, CERTIFIED COLORS AND ARTIFICIAL FLAVORS. NET WEIGHT 1 OZ. MANUFACTURED EXCLUSIVELY BY J. H. MILLSTEIN CO. JEANETTE, PA. 3$\frac{1}{4}$" high, 2$\frac{1}{2}$" long.

(479) Root beer-colored boot is frosted and has straps on each side and wrinkles at the ankle. 3$\frac{1}{4}$" high, 2$\frac{1}{8}$" long.

(480) Aqua iridescent boot with original Imperial Glass label and their ⚜ mark on the sole. 2$\frac{3}{4}$" high, 2$\frac{7}{8}$" long.

(481) Opaque white boot with handpainted decoration in pink and gold. 2$\frac{3}{4}$" high, 2$\frac{3}{4}$" long.

(482) Crystal boot with remains of paint on sole and part of a sticker which reads SOUVENIR OF NATURAL BRIDGE, VA. 2$\frac{5}{8}$" high, 2$\frac{3}{4}$" long.

(483) Black boot shot glass trimmed in silver. On the right side is THIS IS NOT, on the left JUST A SWALLOW over a silver swallow. 2$\frac{5}{8}$" high, 2$\frac{1}{2}$" long.

(484) Crystal boot with ruby-stained top marked COWBOY 1912. 2$\frac{5}{8}$" high, 2$\frac{1}{2}$" long.

(484A) Same as (484), marked IND. STATE FAIR 1949.

(485) Crystal boot from the same mould as (484). Ruby-stained top reads EL PASO. 2$\frac{5}{8}$" high, 2$\frac{1}{2}$" long.

(486) Opaque blue boot. 2$\frac{1}{2}$" high, 2$\frac{1}{2}$" long.

(487) Same as (486). Opaque white.

(488) Opaque white boot marked FRANCE on sole. 2$\frac{1}{2}$" high, 2$\frac{3}{8}$" long.

(489) Crystal boot with stippled strap and spur and "R" on the sole. 2$\frac{1}{2}$" high, 2$\frac{1}{4}$" long.

(490) Crystal boot. Similar to (489) but without strap and spur. 2$\frac{1}{2}$" high, 2$\frac{1}{4}$" long.

(491) Frosted opaque white boot with cuff has original Imperial Glass labels, one reads GENUINE MILK GLASS and the other ORIGINAL DOESKIN FINISH. 2$\frac{3}{4}$" high, 2$\frac{3}{4}$" long.

(492) Same as (488). Pink.

(493) Same as (488). Green.

(494) Crystal boot etched MURPHY REG'D JEWELLER 1461 PEEL ST. Probably English because of the spelling of jeweler. 2$\frac{1}{4}$" high, 2$\frac{1}{2}$" long.

PLATE 39

(495) Blue thimble holder. There is an opening in the shoe which is shaped to hold a thimble. "B.&R." is embossed on the right side. I do not know what it stands for or who made the shoe. Other known colors are crystal (495A), amber and apple green. 4" long, 2⅜" high, c. 1880.

(495A) Same as (495). Crystal.

(496) Same as (495). Amber.

(497) Same as (495). Apple green.

(498) Perfume bottle, crystal over dark green. It has a cut flower and leaf design with cut bands decorating the ankle, toe and heel. The heel was applied separately. The sole and heel have been ground so that the bottle stands securely. It has a metal stopper which is not original. 4½" high, 1¾" long, c. 1890–1920.

(499) Cobalt boot with an elongated foot and decorated in gold. Probably European. Also known in green opaline (499B) (499C) and ruby (499A). 4" long, 2⅜" high, c. 1880s.

(499A) Same as (499). Ruby.

(499B) Same as (499). Green opaline. 2¼" high, 2¾" long.

(499C) Same as (499). Green opaline. Measuring 1½" high, 3⅝" long.

(500) Rose-colored slag boot pitcher has white painted laces. 1½" high, 1⅜" long.

(501) Blue boot pitcher with crystal handle. 1⅝" high, 1⅜" long (including handle).

(502) Yellow boot pitcher with crystal handle. 1¾" high, 1⅜" long.

(503) Red boot pitcher with crystal handle. 1½" high, 1⅜" long.

(504) Small green shoe, Diamond pattern, may have held two perfume bottles. Marked FRANCE. 3" long, 1½" high, c. 1920s.

(505) Same as (504). Peach. Marked FRANCE. Others marked FRANCE were made in light blue, medium green and opaque white.

(506) Lavender shoe with two perfume bottles. Marked JAPAN on the sole and on each bottle. Other shoes marked JAPAN have been found in crystal, gold, pale blue, olive green and root beer. 3" long, c. 1920s.

(507) Brownish-colored shoe with perfume bottles. Only one of the stoppers is original, c. 1920s.

(508) Blue Daisy & Button miniature shoe or salt. Many copies have been made over the years and it is difficult to tell the difference. 3¼" long, 1¾" high.

(509) Aqua miniature shoe in Daisy & Square pattern. Salt collectors consider this to be a salt. 3¼" long, 1¾" high, c. 1880s. Its reproduction is ¼" lower in the back and should create no problem in telling them apart (Fig. 57).

(510) Same as (509). Vaseline.

(511) Same as (509). Dark blue.

(512) Same as (509). Amber.

(513) Same as (509). Blue.

(514) Aqua boot thimble holder, most of which is stippled. It is made to look like a high shoe or boot and the thimble rests in the top in a vertical position. Most shoe thimble holders have the thimbles in a horizontal position. This one is English and rare. Another aqua lady's boot thimble holder (514A) was probably made by the same company. This one is also partly

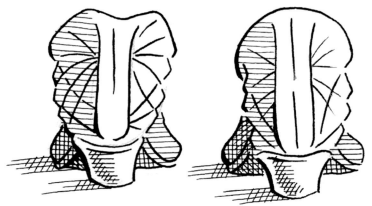

Figure 57. Miniature Daisy & Square shoe. Left, reproduction which is ¼" lower in the back (597). Right, Duncan original (509–515).

PLATE 40

stippled but has wrinkles at the ankle and a large cuff at the top. 1³/₄" high, 1³/₄" long, c. 1880s.

(514A) Similar to (514), probably made by the same company. 2¹/₄" high, 1⁷/₈" long.

(515) Blue thimble holder. These are prized possessions of both shoe and sewing collectors. Some have painted laces, bows or flowers on the vamp and others have only bits of paint remaining to let you know that they had been decorated. Sole and heel are ground. They were made in England. 2³/₈" long, 1¹/₂" high, c. 1880s.

(515A) Same as (515). Black. Original paint is excellent.

(516) Same as (515). Amber with remains of white paint.

(516A) (516B) Same as (516) but different shades.

(517) Same as (515). Dark blue with remains of white paint.

(517A) Same as (517) but a different shade. Original paint is excellent.

(518) Same as (515). Medium green with remains of white paint.

(518A) Same as (518). A different shade of green.

(519) Same as (515). Dark green.

(520) Same as (515). Aqua.

(521) Same as (515). Ruby. Ruby, amethyst and black (515A) are the hardest colors to find.

(522) Opaque white boot, with heel applied separately, has a somewhat crude appearance. The heel, sole and top edge have been ground. 3¹/₈" high, 3³/₈" long.

(523) Opaque white baby bootee, the surface of which looks knitted. It has remains of pink paint and gold trim. Also known in painted blue and painted yellow. 2³/₄" long, 1¹/₂" high, c. 1880.

(524) Opaque white tramp shoe sometimes called a baby shoe. Three toes show through holes in the shoe and it is unlaced. The original shoes are found either left or right and, therefore, can be collected as pairs. They may also be found with either a round depression in the sole or a keyhole-shaped depression. This one has remains of original paint. Right shoe. The shoe was copied by Degenhart from 1962 to 1978 and by Boyd from 1978 but the reproductions are narrower through the foot and the sole edge is more prominent. The old ones were made in opaque white only, while the copies were made in many colors. All the Boyd shoes are marked ◇Ⓑ on the bottom and some of the Degenharts are marked on the inside with Ⓓ. 3" long, 2¹/₈" high, c. 1880.

(525) Same as (524). Left shoe.

(526) Crystal perfume bottle with original label reading EAU DE PARFUM-GREEN SHOES-VIOLET GARDED CORP.-DIST. 2 FL. OZ. This same bottle has been found with different labels. 4¹/₄" high, 3³/₈" long, c. 1920–1930.

(526A) Same as (526) but has a different label. This one reads EAU DE PARFUM EXTRAORDINAIRE-FRENCH SLIPPER-ORIGINAL FRENCH-DISTR. N.Y.-SLIPPER PERF. CO. 2 FL. OZ. A smaller label on the side reads MICHEL D'OR NO. 8.

(527) Crystal shoe in Diamond pattern holds pink and green perfume bottles in the same pattern. The stoppers are original and MADE IN CZECHOSLOVAKIA is acid etched on the sole and on the bottom of each bottle. The shoe was also made in blue and in pink. The glass is of good quality. The shoe is 3" long, 1¹/₂" high without the bottles. Each bottle is 2" high to the top of the stopper, c. 1920–30.

(528) Crystal cut-glass boot scent bottle, heel applied separately, heel and sole ground. 2⅛" high, c. 1880–1900.

(528A) Same as (528) but with different pattern, measuring 3" high.

(528B) Same as (528) but with different pattern, measuring 3¼" high.

(528C) Same as (528) but with different pattern, measuring 2¼" high.

(529) Crystal cut-glass boot scent bottle, heel applied separately, heel and sole ground. 3⅛" high, c. 1880–1900.

(530) Crystal cut-glass boot scent bottle, heel applied separately, heel and sole ground. 3¼" high, c. 1880–1900.

(531) Blown crystal boot perfume. 3¼" high, c. 1880.

(532) Crystal whimsey with a hand and five fingers at one end, a foot with five toes at the other and latticino in the center from the toes to the tips of the fingers. In addition, there is an opalescent spiral the entire length. 3⅞" high.

(533) Crystal cut-glass boot scent bottle, heel applied separately, heel and sole ground. 3⅛" high, c. 1880–1900.

(533A) Similar to (533). This bottle has a silver neck and a small crystal stopper. The upper part is wider than most of the cut-glass boot scent bottles. It measures 3½" to top of the stopper.

(533B) Similar to (533). Blue, which is a rare color, since boot scent bottles are almost always crystal. 2⅝" to top of neck.

(534) Opaque white shoe stickpin. Shoe has scalloped top edge and is ⅞" long.

(535) Blown crystal boot perfume. 2⅝" high, c. 1880.

(536) Same as (509). Crystal Daisy & Square miniature shoe or salt.

(537) Same as (508). Crystal Daisy & Button miniature shoe or salt.

(538) Crystal attached pair of shoes. Used as a salt. Also made in opaque white (538A). 2¾" long, 2" wide, 1¼" high, c. 1880.

(538A) Same as (538). Opaque white.

(539) Similar to (527). Same crystal Cube pattern but the clear portion on the vamp is shaped differently. This shoe has been found with a round paper label marked MADE IN CHINA. 3" long, 1½" high.

(540) Shoe made with glass beads and wire. Crystal, amber, blue and red beads. 3" long, c. 1900.

(541) Spun glass shoe. 2" long, 2¼" high.

(542) Same as (515). Crystal thimble holder with painted flowers.

(542A) Same as (542) but with original painting in excellent condition, especially the wading bird on the front. 2⅜" long, 1½" high.

(543) Spun glass shoe. 1⅝" long, 1¾" high.

(544) Spun glass shoe. 1⅞" long, 1½" high.

(545) Crystal thimble holder, marked ⑂ for the Thimble Society of London. Three glass buttons on each side of the front opening. 2⅜" long, 1½" high, c. 1985.

(546) Same as (545), with two blue buttons on each side of opening. 2½" long, 1½" high, c. 1985.

(547) Frosted crystal thimble holder/pincushion with silver toe and band around top. English. 3⅜" long, 1⅛" high.

(547A) Same as (547), blue. The shoe has gold writing on the front reading CHICAGO 1893 for the Columbian Exposition. It probably also had a pincushion on top when it was new.

(547B) Same as (547). This shoe is painted black with a sterling silver toe and has a pincushion which may or may not be the original.

(548) Grey/white slag boot pitcher. 1½" high, foot is 1⅜" long.

(549) Pink/white slag boot pitcher. Also made in yellow/white slag, opaque orange and opaque red. 1½" high, foot is 1⅜" long.

PLATE 41

(550) Same as (479). Crystal frosted man's boot. Straps on each side with stitching detail. 3¹/₈" high, 2¹/₂" long.

(551) Crystal cuffed boot with turned-up toe. Also known in amber, cobalt (551B), amethyst (551A) and green. A silver and black paper label reads KUMELA RIIHIMÄKI MADE IN FINLAND. 2³/₄" high, 2¹/₂" long.

(551A) Same as (551). Amethyst.

(551B) Same as (551). Cobalt.

(552) Crystal boot salt shaker on round rayed base but rays do not extend to the edge. Decorated with shield and lightly stippled at top. Possibly made at the time of the Centennial in 1876. 3³/₈" high without metal top.

(553) Crystal boot salt shaker on shell-shaped base. Shield is different shape than (552) and foot is wider. 3¹/₄" high without top, c. 1876.

(554) Crystal boot with mustard jar top. Shield is different shape than either (552) or (553) and rays on round base extend to the edge. 3¹/₂" high without top, c. 1876.

(555) Crystal shoe cologne bottle has raised design on front of all sizes. This type of shoe cologne was made by Kastrup Glassworks near Copenhagen, Denmark, and shown at a DANISH GLASS 1814–1914 exhibit at the Victoria and Albert Museum in London in 1974 (Fig. 58). The sole and heel are slightly indented. Marked "LM" on the sole. Because the necks vary in length, I will give the measurement of the flat portion on top and then the overall length. 2³/₈"–5¹/₂" c. 1886.

(556) Same as (555). Marked "LM" on sole. 1⁷/₈"–4¹/₂".

(557) Same as (555). Marked "LM" on sole. 1³/₈"–3⁵/₈".

(558) Crystal shoe cologne. Plain except for laced front. Marked "R&M" on sole. 1¹/₄"–3⁵/₈".

(559) Crystal shoe cologne with small flowers and ribbon on front. Original label on top marked ROSE OIL. The same type of bottle, with a label on top, is shown in the Spring 1886 Spelman Brothers

Figure 58. *(Left)* This shoe cologne bottle (555) was part of the Danish Glass exhibit at the Victoria and Albert Museum in London, 1974. Courtesy of the Rakow Library, Corning Museum of Glass.

Figure 59. *(Below)* Advertisement from the Spring 1886 Spelman Brothers Wholesale Catalog.

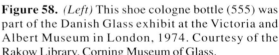
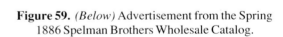

5, 10 and 25 CENT PERFUMERIES.

No.	No. 162.	DOZ.	GROSS.
162.	Slipper Cologne	$0 40	$4 50
202.	Slipper Hair Oil	40	4 50
163.	Boot Cologne	45	5 25
203.	Boot Hair Oil	.45	5 25
204.	Cologne Horse-shoe Bottles	50	5 50
205.	Cologne, in fancy bottles	75	8 75
207.	Mirror Cologne	83	9 50
206.	Large Boot Cologne	80	9 50
208.	Wood Scoop, with bottle of Cologne	95	11 00
209.	Colored glass Tub, with bottle of Cologne	1 00	11 50

PLATE 42

Wholesale Catalog (Fig. 59). It was advertised as HALL'S DIME COLOGNE. 2"–4⅝", c. 1880s. Also see Butler Brothers *Cold Weather Edition "Our Drummer" Catalog* from January 1888 (Fig. 55). One size was advertised at 43¢ per dozen wholesale. This bottle comes in at least six sizes.

(559A) Similar to (559). 2" long on top, 4⅞" overall length.

(560) Same as (559). 2¼"–5¼".

(561) Same as (559). 2½"–5⅞".

(561A) Similar to (561). 5¾" overall length.

(562) Same as (559). 1⅝"–3⅞".

(563) Same as (559). 1¼"–3½".

(563A) Similar to (563) but instead of a flower and ribbon on the front, this cologne bottle has a small buckle and ribbon. Flat portion of top is 1¼", overall length is 3½".

(564) Same as (559). 1⅛"–2⅞".

(565) Ruby cocktail shaker in a silver-colored metal sandal whose straps are covered with a star design. There are silver scrolls on the sides and vamp of the shaker and the band around the top is also silver. The cover is chrome with a vented strainer which has a screw-on lid. The cover is marked DERBY SHELTON SILVER CO. SHELTON, CONN. PAT. 2091604. The patent was granted on August 31, 1937, and has to do with proper venting of the cover so that an airlock will not form when pouring the contents. Sometimes the pouring spout is set at an angle and not straight up. It is pictured in *Victorian Glass* without the sandal or cover and rests on a heel of wood covered with kid. It is 12½" high to top of leg, 15⅜" high to top of cover and shoe is 6¾" long.

Six matching glasses, each with silver bands around the top and bottom, complete the set. 3³⁄₁₆" high.

This shaker was also made in etched crystal with matching stems (565A) and frosted crystal with matching glasses (565B). I have read that it was also made in cobalt but have been unable to confirm this. The maker was West Virginia Specialty Glass, c. 1937.

(565A) Same as (565), but this cocktail shaker is etched crystal and came with matching crystal stems.

(565B) Same as (565), this cocktail shaker is frosted crystal. The pouring spout is set at an angle. Has matching glasses with silver edge on the top and bottom.

APPLIED RIGAREE

(772) This wonderful crystal shoe is mould blown with an all over Diamond pattern. It has an applied cranberry ribbon with a raspberry on the front. The sole, heel and top edge have all been ground. It is quite heavy for its size, weighing 1 pound, 3 ounces. This rare shoe was purchased in England. Measures 6$^3/_4$" long, 3$^1/_8$" high.

(773) This crystal slipper with blue threading and applied crystal rigaree round the top edge was purchased in England. The heel and sole have been polished. 5" long, 2$^3/_4$" high.

(774) Blown crystal shoe with an opaque blue rigaree around the opening. This is unusual since applied rigaree is usually done in crystal. It has a polished pontil on the heel. Purchased in England. 5$^1/_4$" long, 3" high.

(775) Opalescent vaseline blown shoe with applied vaseline rigaree around the top edge. Purchased in England. 3$^5/_8$" long, 2$^3/_8$" high.

(776) Blown crystal miniature shoe with applied crystal rigaree. It is unusual to find a shoe this small with applied rigaree. The heel and sole are ground. Purchased in England. 2$^1/_2$" long, 1$^1/_2$" high.

(777) Another blown crystal miniature shoe with applied crystal rigaree. The heel and sole are ground. Purchased in England. Measures 2$^1/_2$" long, 1$^3/_4$" high.

VENETIAN

(778) This shoe has alternating stripes of white and rose in crystal, ruffled edge. 5" long, 2$^1/_8$" high.

(779) The sole of this shoe is white latticino, and the front is twisted latticino in white, blue, pink and green. There are two applied flowers on the front, and a ruffled edge. 5$^1/_2$" long, 2$^1/_4$" high.

(780) Both the sole and the front are made of rows of twisted white latticino and twisted green ribbon. A crystal glass bow on the front is a somewhat unusual decoration. 5$^1/_2$" long, 2$^1/_4$" high.

(781) The sole on this shoe consists of alternating stripes of amber and white. The top is made of stripes of white and twisted aqua. The heel and the ruffles are a pale pink. Measures 6$^1/_8$" long, 2$^1/_8$" high.

(782) This shoe has a white latticino sole, and is covered on top with twisted green ribbons. The top edge looks scalloped instead of the usual ruffle, and the heel is black and gold instead of crystal. 4$^5/_8$" long, 1$^5/_8$" high.

(783) The top of this shoe is crystal, white and goldstone, and the ruffle is crystal. The sole is white and crystal. 5$^1/_4$" long, 2" high.

(784) This shoe has a red sole, and the usual crystal heel and ruffle. The upper portion has twisted blue ribbons. 4$^5/_8$" long, 1$^1/_2$" high.

(785) All white latticino shoe with a yellow heel and rolled top edge. 4" long, 1$^1/_2$" high.

(786) All blue latticino shoe with a crystal ruffled top edge. The heel is very unusual in that it is just a round, flat piece of glass. This is the only Venetian shoe I have ever seen with the heel done this way. 4$^3/_4$" long, 1$^3/_8$" high.

(787) This shoe is dark green and white millefiore with a crystal ruffle and heel. Measures 5$^3/_4$" long, 2$^3/_8$" high.

(788) This interesting blue Venetian shoe is cased white on the inside, with a Diamond Quilted pattern on the outside. On top of the pattern, it is frosted all over. The sole contains the same pattern as the rest of the shoe. Measures 7$^1/_4$" long, 2$^1/_2$" high.

(789) Small Italian boot with turned-up toe, gold opalescent. 3$^1/_4$" high, 3$^3/_8$" long.

(790) Small Italian boot with turned-up toe, green opalescent with various other colors. It also has indentations on the front which look like buttons. 2$^3/_4$" high, 3$^1/_4$" long.

(791) Venetian glass boot with alternating stripes of white latticino and twisted ribbons in green, blue, pink and yellow. The heel is black and gold. 3$^3/_8$" high, 3$^3/_4$" long.

(792) This shoe was purchased at a flea market in 1996. I would have assumed it to be Italian had it not been for the paper label which reads ICET ARTE MURANO HECHO IN VENEZUELA. Apparently, someone—or some company—is, or was making Murano-type shoes in Venezuela. 6" long, 2" high.

GILLINDER

(793) This opaque white Gillinder shoe, sometimes called the Centennial shoe, was made continuously from the 1870s until the 1890s. It was shown on an undated "Sundries" page from a Gillinder & Sons catalog, simply called "Slipper" (Fig. 64). Frank Leslie's *Illustrated Historical Register of the Centennial Exposition* (1876) includes a short article on the exhibition glass house constructed and sponsored by Gillinder & Sons. While at the Exposition, the factory sold "enormous quantities" of various glass articles engraved with "Centennial 1876," among them these "pretty little glass slippers." Scarce in opaque white, 5½" long, 2½" high.

(794) Vaseline Gillinder shoe, the same as (90) (95) (97). This shoe is rare in vaseline, and is the only one I know of.

(795) Another Gillinder shoe, the same color blue as (97). This one is contained inside a silver-colored metal webbing. Scarce.

(796) This amber Gillinder is the same as (95), but like (795) it is covered with a metal webbing. The metal on this shoe is not shiny.

(797) Vertical ribbed Gillinder similar to (134), but this color is much more turquoise. Trimmed in gold, 4¼" high, 4¼" long. This shoe appeared on an undated "Sundries" page from a Gillinder & Sons catalog, called "Boot No. 2" (Fig. 64).

(798) Another Gillinder high shoe, same as (141–142) (151). Vaseline. This shoe appeared on an undated "Sundries" page from a Gillinder & Sons catalog, called "Boot No. 1" (Fig. 64).

(799) This is the same high shoe as (151). It is in a metal skate which is a perfect fit for the shoe. The oval base, which measures 4⅜" long, 2⅝" wide, is silver-plated and marked PAT. APPLD. FOR MORGAN SILVER CO. The wheels on the skate turn.

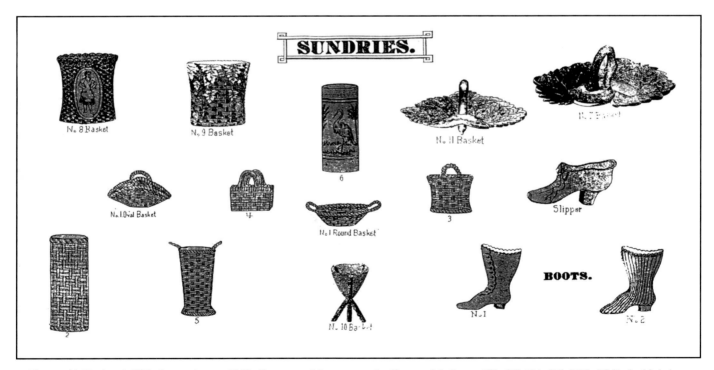

Figure 64. Undated Gillinder catalog, c. 1880. Shown on this page are the Centennial slipper (89–91) (94–97) (793–794), the high-button boot (141–142) (151) (798), and the ribbed boot (128–129) (134) (797). This catalog page is significant in that it confirmed the definite maker of these shoes. While the two Boot drawings were illustrated in Ruth Webb Lee's book *Victorian Glass*, I now know the drawings came from this Gillinder catalog page. Courtesy of the Jones Museum of Glass & Ceramics, The Edward W. Tinney Memorial Library.

HIGH-BUTTON STYLE

(800) Beautiful amberina high shoe with eleven buttons on the left side and large beading around the top edge. There are vertical ribs on the inside of the upper portion and the sole has horizontal ridges which may be seen in the photo. This shoe may possibly be a Gillinder since it is similar to the ribbed shoe (141–142) (151) (798). 4½" high, 3¾" long.

(801) Plain opaque white high shoe, with no pattern, markings or etching. This shoe was recently acquired and I know of no other just like it. 4¼" high, 4³⁄₈" long.

(802) This crystal high shoe is painted red on the inside and the surface is both plain and stippled. There are ten buttons on each side and the sole and heel are hollow. Measures 4⅛" high, 3⅝" long.

CLOGS

(803) Crystal clog with turned-up toe has metal around the top edge, on the bottom of the heel, and on the toe. This shoe was mould blown, and allowance was made in the mould for the metal to fit flush with the glass. The metal work is very well done. Measures 4⅞" long, 2⅛" high.

(804) Blue clog with five white painted buttons on the front and no other decorations at all. The glass is thick and the shoe is heavy for its size. 4³⁄₈" long, 1¾" high.

(805) Attached pair of purple/white slag clogs. Each shoe has a bow with short streamers but no other decoration. This was purchased in England. The shoes measure 4⅝" long, 1³⁄₈" high, 2⅝" wide.

MINIATURES

(806) Small crystal blown shoe with white painted laces and a white painted decorative edge around the opening. Possibly meant to be a thimble holder. 2¾" long, 1¼" high.

(807) Small, solid amber glass shoe that appears to be cut and polished. 1⅞" long, ¾" high.

(808) Same as (806).

(809) Small, turquoise-blue blown shoe with applied heel and applied black bow. 3⅛" long, 2½" high.

(810) Small, blue opaline shoe that has been polished all over including the sole and heel. It is decorated with gold and white enamel. 3¼" long, ⅝" high.

(811) Same as (809).

(812) Blown shoe in crystal over cranberry. 3¼" long, 1¾" high.

MEN'S SHOES

(813) Small man's shoe, crystal over cranberry, with the remains of gold decoration and a very pointed toe. 3³⁄₈" long, 1" high.

(814) Crystal cut glass man's shoe with wonderful details which include laces across the front. This shoe is a match box holder and could have been used as an ashtray or as a paperweight since it is quite heavy. Purchased in England. 6½" long, 2" high to top of shoe, 2½" high to top of match box holder.

(815) Crystal, clear and frosted golf shoe paperweight. This shoe has a frosted "ghillie" tongue and toe. There are five cleats on the sole and three on the heel. The sticker reads MAGIC CRYSTAL-MADE IN WEST GERMANY. It was purchased new in 1992. 5⅞" long, 2¾" high.

(816) Crystal golf shoe with WATERFORD CRYSTAL-MADE IN IRELAND on a green and gold paper sticker. It also has an acid-etched WATERFORD on the bottom of the heel. Used as a paperweight, this piece is very heavy. Purchased new in 1996. 5¾" long, 2¼" high.

(817) Crystal tennis shoe paperweight. 5⅝" long, 2⅛" high.

SCENTS AND COLOGNES

(818) Crystal cut glass shoe perfume bottle which appears to have all the original parts. This was purchased in England. 4³/₈" long, 3" high to the top of the glass.

(819) Early swirled glass scent bottle. 3⁷/₈" high, c. 1820–50.

(820) Blown, teal-colored scent bottle with large neck. Purchased in England. 3⁵/₈" high.

(821) Painted glass leg with red shoe and metal cap marked GERMANY. The leg is attached to the original advertising card which reads PER-FUMERY and CUSSONS-LONDON & MAN-CHESTER-MADE IN ENGLAND. The metal cap is in the shape of a crown and the whole piece, including the stopper, measures 3¹/₂". Circa 1920s.

(822) Same as (820).

(823) This small green scent bottle is frosted on the bottom. The top consists of eight vertical panels and the neck is slightly damaged. 2¹/₄" high, foot is 1¹/₂" long.

(824) Man's work shoe perfume bottle, with only traces of gold paint. The cap is at the back and has a red and white tassel attached. There are tiny hobnails on the sole and heel. 3¹/₈" long including the cap, 1⁵/₈" high.

(825) Same as (824), but with gold paint intact.

(826) Small cologne/perfume bottle with the neck opening at the back. This bottle has a lightly stippled surface and three button holes on each side at the front. 3¹/₂" long to the end of the neck, 1¹/₂" high.

(827) Cologne/perfume bottle shaped like a clog. The opening is at the back and has a metal cap on a threaded neck. The top half is painted gold. Measures 3" long including the cap, 1" high.

(828) Clog-shaped cologne/perfume opens at the back with a black cap on a threaded neck. There is a small curved, decorative band across the front. Measures 3¹/₄" long including cap, 1" high.

FLASKS

Most of the flasks discussed here were made circa the 19th century.

(829) Nailsea-type boot flask, crystal with white looping. 9" high, 4" wide, foot is 3" long.

(830) Nailsea-type boot flask, cranberry with white looping. Colored glass, such as the cranberry, is much harder to find with looping than crystal glass. This flask was purchased in England. 7¹/₂" high, 3³/₄" wide, foot is 2³/₈" long.

(831) Nailsea-type boot flask, crystal with white looping. Measures 8⁵/₈" high, 3³/₄" wide; the foot is 3" long.

(832) A somewhat rounder Nailsea-type boot flask with wide white looping. Purchased in England. 6¹/₂" high, 3³/₈" wide, foot is 2" long.

(833) A short Nailsea-type boot flask in crystal with wide white looping. Purchased in England. 5" high, 2¹/₂" wide, foot is 2¹/₈" long.

(834) Boot flask with cranberry, yellow-green and opalescent spiral stripes. Unfortunately the photo does not do justice to the colors. 7" high, 3¹/₂" wide, foot is 2⁷/₈" long.

(835) Light green spiral opalescent boot flask. Purchased in England. 7³/₄" high, 3¹/₂" wide, foot is 2³/₄" long.

(836) Crystal over blue boot flask. Purchased in England. Measures 5⁷/₈" high, 3³/₈" wide; foot is 2¹/₂" long.

(837) Opalescent crystal boot flask with white spirals. 9" high, 4³/₄" wide, foot is 2¹/₄" long.

(838) Spiral crystal boot flask purchased in England. 6⁵/₈" high, 3³/₄" wide, foot is 2" long.

(839) Small plain crystal boot flask with original stopper. Both neck and stopper are ground. The initial "R" is etched on one side. Purchased in England. 5³/₄" high to the top of the stopper, 2⁷/₈" wide, foot is 1¹/₂" long.

(840) Crystal over amber boot flask. 6³/₄" high, 3¹/₄" wide, foot is 2⁷/₈" long.

(841) Crystal over cranberry boot flask. 7⁵/₈" high, 4" wide, foot is 1³/₄" long.

(842) Crystal over cranberry boot flask. 8¹/₂" high, 3³/₄" wide, foot is 2⁵/₈" long.

CUT GLASS BOOTS

(843) Wonderful cut glass boot with spur. Possibly Russian, purchased in Paris. Crystal, 5³/₄" high, 4³/₄" long.

(844) Cut glass boot with applied heel. Crystal, 7⁵/₈" high, 5" long.

(845) Cut glass boot with applied heel. Crystal, 7¹/₂" high, 5³/₈" long.

(846) Steuben cut glass boot with acid-etched mark on the heel (Fig. 65), c. 1903–32. Pattern has four small diamonds forming a larger diamond, all enclosed in an even larger diamond. 10³/₄" high, 6¹/₄" long.

(847) Crystal cut glass boot has square toe and applied heel. The pattern on the top third of the boot is repeated three more times. Measures 11" high, 7" long.

(848) Crystal cut glass boot with flowers on the front and back, and leaves on the sides. The heel is applied and there is a label which reads CRYSTAL, MOUTH BLOWN, HAND CUT. 9¹/₈" high, 6" long.

(849) Large cut glass boot with applied heel. The heel and sole have been ground. Measures 10⁷/₈" high, 6" long.

(850) Cut glass boot, green cut back to crystal. A similar boot was also made in ruby (566) and blue (568). This boot may also be seen as (566A). 7³/₄" high, 5¹/₂" long.

Figure 65. The acid-etched mark appearing on Steuben cut glass boot (845), used c. 1903–32. A reproduction mark has been identified, with more modern lettering, and the "S" touching the top of the banner. From Anne Geffken Pullen's *Glass Signatures, Trademarks and Trade Names*, p. 306, used by permission from Krause Publications.

SMALL BOOTS

(851) This small crystal boot on an oval pedestal is somewhat heavy for its size. It is shown in Ruth Webb Lee's *Victorian Glass*, with a frosted finish. 3³/₄" high, 3⁵/₈" long, c. 1880s.

(852) This small crystal boot is solid glass almost up to the frosted area, and it has a silver band around the top edge. Purchased in England. 2¹/₂" high, 2¹/₂" long.

(853) Small crystal boot with gold bands that have been etched with grapes and grape leaves. 5⁷/₈" high, 4" long.

(854) Same as (853), but 4¹/₄" high and 2⁷/₈" long.

(855) Same as (853), but 3" high and 1⁷/₈" long. This one has ROTHENBURG in gold lettering at the top edge.

(856) Stippled and smooth crystal boot. The foot portion, which has the strap and spur, is smooth. The middle of the boot, which includes the rings, is stippled and the top is smooth. 3" high, 1⁷/₈" long.

(857) Small crystal boot with straps and wrinkles above the ankle. This boot is a copy of the original (858). 3¹/₈" high, 1³/₄" long.

(858) Small crystal boot with straps and wrinkles above the ankle. This boot has a hollow foot, polished top edge and is made of much better quality glass than (857). 3³/₈" high, 1⁷/₈" long.

(859) Small frosted cowboy boot. Measures 3⁷/₈" high, 2⁷/₈" long.

(860) Crystal cowboy boot with RALPH LAUREN acid etched on the sole. The sole and heel are polished and the boot is solid glass and quite heavy. 5" high, 3⁷/₈" long.

(861) Attached pair of opaque black boots. 2¹/₂" high.

MEDIUM BOOTS

(862) Crystal over cranberry Bohemian boot with an applied heel. There are gold and white enameled flowers on the front and back. 7" high, 5¼" long, c. 1840–60.

(863) Crystal over cranberry boot has enameled decorations all over. The top edge and heel are trimmed in gold. 6⅝" high, 2⅞" long.

(864) Cobalt boot is covered with painted flowers and leaves. The name ALASSIO is painted on. 6⅝" high, 4⅛" long.

(865) Crystal over dark, dark red. This boot is decorated with silver and gold enamel, including on the square-cut toe. Label reads MADE IN GERMAN DEMOCRATIC REPUBLIC. 6¼" high, 3⅛" long.

(866) Crystal with white looping. This Nailsea-type boot has a red rim. 8½" high, 2½" long.

(867) This Nailsea-type boot is crystal with white looping. 6⅛" high, 2½" long.

(868) Ruby-stained boot with a strap and the top edge in gold. FEDONA 1877 is etched on one side and CARLY is on the other side. 6" high, 3⅞" long.

(869) Crystal boot with applied heel. On the front, etched flowers surround the name JOHN COTTRELL and on the back is "gew. von Dr. Vollmer u. Frau." 7½" high, 4⅝" long.

(870) Yellow stippled boot trimmed in gold. There is a decal on the front which reads KOBLENZ DEUTCHES ECK. 6¼" high, 3¾" long.

Figure 66. Medium crystal boot with spiral ribs on the upper portion, and wrinkles down to the ankle. The foot is plain with a nicely done strap with a buckle. 5⅞" high, 4" long.

Figure 67. Medium crystal boot with an etched thistle and leaves. The top edge is scalloped. On the back is JOHN O' GROATS, on the northern tip of Scotland. 5¼" high, 3⅝" long.

(871) Crystal boot with ruby-stained upper portion (2¹/₈" wide). White flowers have been hand-painted over the stain. 7³/₈" high, 4³/₈" long.

(872) The entire boot is amber cut back to crystal. The front portion of the sole has a diamond pattern. 5³/₄" high, 3¹/₈" long.

(873) Frosted crystal over ruby boot. RIVIERA ADRIATICA in white enamel decorates the boot. 6³/₄" high, 4" long.

(874) Crystal over cranberry boot is decorated with white enamel flowers and gold. Measures 9" high, 6³/₄" long.

(875) Blown crystal boot with a rough pontil on the heel. The foot portion was added on, and there are rigaree straps on each side at the top. 7¹/₂" high, 5³/₈" long.

(876) The top half of this boot is amber cut to clear, and shows a bear within a shield. Underneath is the word BERLIN. 6¹/₄" high, 3⁷/₈" long.

(877) Same as (876) with the top half also amber cut to clear. Around the top are the words FRO-BELTURM OBERWEISSBACH THUR-WALD. 6¹/₄" high, foot is 3³/₄" long.

(878) Crystal boot with metal strap and spur. There is a diamond pattern etched around the top with straight lines below it. 9³/₈" high, 8¹/₂" high from toe to spur tip.

(879) Green boot of very thin glass has a fluted edge and a strap at the ankle. Purchased in England, 5⁷/₈" high, 4³/₈" long.

(880) Amethyst boot with spirals that are more pronounced on the inside. Purchased in England, 5⁷/₈" high, 4³/₈" long.

(881) Same as (879) in turquoise.

(882) This boot is from the same mould as (195) (197), with buttons on the right and different etching. It looks as if it was intended to be a vase. 7¹/₈" high, the base is 4" in diameter.

(883) Similar to (882), this boot has buttons on the left so it was made from a different mould.

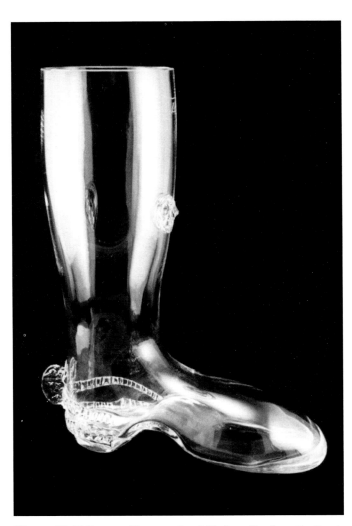

Figure 68. Tall crystal boot makred 1L (one liter) on the front, about an inch from the top. The heel is applied and has a row of rigaree above it. There is also an applied strap, spur and a small decoration on the front. 10¹/₄" high, 7" long.

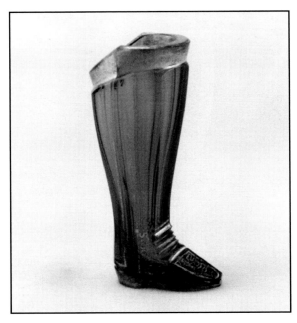

Figure 69. Very attractive eight-sided boot, decorated with gold. The heel and sole have been polished. This boot, or a similar one, was illustrated in an article by Jane Shadel Spillman in *Spinning Wheel* magazine, March/April 1981 (see Fig. 72). It measures 3³/₈" high, 1³/₈" long.

STIRRUP CUPS

(884) Blown Nailsea-type stirrup cup in crystal with white looping. Purchased in England, 3⁷/₈" high, 1³/₄" long.

(885) Another blown Nailsea-type stirrup cup in crystal with white looping. Purchased in England, 4¹/₂" high, 2³/₄" long.

(886) Blown crystal stirrup cup with etched leaves and marked A. BROWN 1884. Purchased in England, 2⁷/₈" high, 2¹/₄" long.

(887) Blown opalescent stirrup cup with applied green threading. 4" high, 2³/₈" long.

(888) Blown opalescent vaseline stirrup cup. Purchased in England, 4³/₈" high, 2" long.

(889) Blown crystal over cranberry stirrup cups, measuring 3³/₄" high.

(890) Blown crystal over cranberry stirrup cup has vertical ribs. Purchased in England, 3⁵/₈" high, 1¹/₂" long.

(891) Blown cobalt stirrup cup has the pontil mark on the heel. Purchased in England, measuring 4" high, 2¹/₄" long.

(892) Swirled crystal stirrup cup with the pontil mark on the heel. Purchased in England, measuring 4³/₄" high, 2¹/₂" long.

(893) Blown crystal stirrup cup with very attractive etching around the top. 4¹/₂" high, 2³/₈" long.

(894) Blown crystal stirrup cup with a diamond pattern cut around the top. There are horizontal cuts down the back to the heel and cuts all around the sole edge. Purchased in England, 3⁵/₈" high, 2³/₈" long.

(895) Blown crystal stirrup cup. The top 1¹/₄" is frosted except for the front where the initials R.S. have been etched. England, 3⁷/₈" high, 2¹/₄" long.

Figure 70. Crystal over amethyst stirrup with an applied heel. It has a silvery finish on the heel, toe and around the top edge. The finish shows better on a darker colored glass. 3¹/₂" high, 2" long.

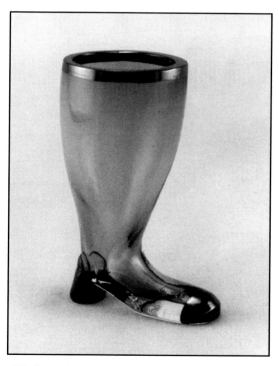

Figure 71. Crystal over green stirrup with an applied heel. It has a silvery finish on the heel, toe and around the top edge. Measures 3¹/₂" high, 2" long.

(896) Blown crystal stirrup cup. Part of the top is frosted and "WF to PS" is etched on the front. Purchased in England, 4" high, 2³⁄₈" long.

(897) Small, blown crystal stirrup cup. It has a light green applied foot, the only example I have ever seen of an applied foot in a different color. Purchased in England, 3" high, 1⁵⁄₈" long.

(898) This blown crystal boot is unusual in that the bottom half is solid glass while the top half is quite round. Purchased in England, 3¹⁄₈" high, 1" long.

(899) Plain stirrup cup, measuring 3³⁄₈" high, 1³⁄₄" long. Purchased in England.

(900) Slightly larger than (898), this stirrup cup has an applied strip of glass from the top edge to the heel. The strip is horizontally ribbed. Purchased in England, 4¹⁄₈" high, 1⁷⁄₈" long.

(901) Large, blown crystal stirrup cup with applied foot and pontil mark on the heel. Measuring 5¹⁄₄" high, 3" long.

Figure 72. This picture shows a group of small drinking boots or stirrup cups from the Strauss Collection, the Corning Museum of Glass. It is taken from an article written by Jane Shadel Spillman, Curator of American Glass, that appeared in *Spinning Wheel* magazine, March/April 1981. The boot in the center closely resembles Fig. 69, eight-sided boot, decorated with gold. The heel and sole have been polished.

DRINKING BOOTS AND BOOT/SHOE BOTTLES

(902) Blown drinking boot with applied foot. The top two inches are frosted and the initials TB have been etched on the front. 6½" high, 4½" long. The diameter at the top is 3½".

(903) Blown cobalt drinking boot with applied foot. 5⅝" high, 3" long.

(904) Blown, swirled drinking boot with applied foot. 7¼" high, 3¾" long. The diameter at the top measures 3⅝".

(905) Crystal boy in frosted crystal boot. The boy is holding a gun and his hat is the stopper. This was probably made in France, since it is marked DEPOSE on the sole. Measures 11½" high, 5" long.

(906) This large crystal Dutch shoe bottle has a raised leaf design on the front and sides. The shoe stands on the rear of the heel, which contains the pontil mark. 10⅝" high.

(907) Same as (905) but frosted crystal.

(908) Carnival glass bottle of leg and shoe on hassock. Not nearly as old or as nice as (572) (581). 7⅜" high, 2¾" diameter.

(909) Same as (907) but in blue.

(910) Cobalt blue shoe bottle. The foot portion is ribbed and the top looks as though it originally had a cap or cover. The raised lettering at the top left reads H. BERNARD PARIS. On the right side, it is marked DEPOSE. The ribbed portion appears to be identical to the Gillinder high shoe (128), both shoes having 34 ribs. Purchased in England, 4⅜" high, 3¼" long.

(911) This crystal cat in a shoe bottle has the remains of the original COLOGNE label on its neck. In raised letters, the sole is marked TRADE MARK with a larger "T" underneath the words. 3⅞" high, 3½" long.

(912) This very unique bottle is covered with the Old Woman in the Shoe and her children. 3⅜" high, 3⅞" long.

(913) This crystal bottle has a very unusual shape. My guess is that it originally held cologne or perfume. 2⅞" long, 1½" high.

(914) Man's glass shoe decanter with original stopper. The shoe has laces and stitching, and some of the ivory-colored glass has been painted tan and brown to resemble a real shoe. There is a metal collar which has holders for the six cordial glasses. 7¼" long, 5⅜" high without the stopper.

SPOON HOLDERS

(915) Crystal Daisy & Button spoon holder. 7³/₈" long, 2³/₈" high, c. 1880s.

(916) Same as (914) in blue.

(917) Same as (914) in vaseline.

(918) Light olive green Daisy & Button spoon holder, same as (914). This did not fluoresce under a black light as did the vaseline (916). This spoon holder was also made in amber.

(919) Cut glass spoon holder, different from (914–17), which are pressed glass. I consider this to be a rare piece. 9¹/₂" long, 2¹/₄" high.

CONDIMENT SETS

(920) This lovely cut glass shoe holds five pieces of a condiment set, each of which fits in only one place. Not even the salt and pepper shakers can be reversed. The other three pieces are for vinegar, oil and mustard. 7⁵/₈" long, 5¹/₄" high to top of cruet. The shoe itself is 1³/₄" high.

(921) Same Diamond pattern cut glass shoe as (920) but a smaller size. I believe it held a three-piece condiment set, consisting of a salt shaker, pepper shaker and mustard jar. Unfortunately, these pieces did not accompany the shoe! Purchased in England, measuring 6" long, 1¹/₂" high.

(922) Small pressed glass cruet set containing salt and pepper shakers and a mustard jar. The three pieces must be in a specific arrangement to fit. 4⁷/₈" long, 3¹/₄" high to top of shaker. The shoe is 1³/₄" high.

(923) This crystal shoe with a bow on the front holds salt and pepper shakers with silver-colored metal tops. All are pressed glass in a Diamond pattern and each piece is marked FOREIGN. 3¹/₄" long, 3" high to top of shakers.

(924) Diamond pattern pressed glass shoe holding salt and pepper shakers with metal tops. Each shaker is marked JAPAN on the bottom. 3¹/₄" long, 3" high to the top of the shakers.

(925) Diamond pattern pressed glass shoe holding salt and pepper shakers with glass tops. Each shaker is marked JAPAN on the bottom. 3" long, 2¹/₂" high to the top of the shakers.

MISCELLANEOUS

(926) Blue blown glass, short boot with controlled bubbles. While the glass was still pliable, it was cut in two places and that portion was pulled down. The heel and sole are polished and the shoe is quite heavy weighing 1 pound, 12 ounces. Purchased in England. Measures 6" long, 5³/₈" high.

(927) Small blown cased shoe with a ground pontil mark on the heel. The inside is creamy white and the outside is pink at the bottom becoming dark red at the top. Purchased in England, 4" long, 2" high.

(928) This purple/white slag bootee has a mostly stippled surface except for a smooth toe area. It has laces and five lace holes on each side. The heel and sole are hollow. Scarce shoe, also known in crystal. 3³/₈" long, 2" high.

(929) Pink Libbey shoe with a transfer of George Washington on the front and beneath that is the date 1776. It may well have been made for the Centennial as a souvenir. Measures 6¹/₄" long, 3¹/₄" high.

INTRODUCTION TO COLOR PLATES

The following color plates contain shoes that have been found over the last ten years, many of which are rare or one of a kind. A few of them represent unique variations on similar moulds shown in Book One, differing in color, style or decoration. However, in most cases they are new finds which have been discovered since the publication of *Shoes of Glass* in 1988.

There is little or no information available about many of these shoes; however I have provided all I know concerning each shoe's source, markings, physical description and maker.

Each illustrated shoe or boot has been given a number, which can be used to reference a description and a value. In this color section, the numbers are located in the caption underneath each photo.

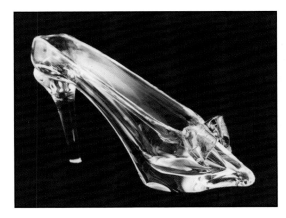

(745) Teal-colored high heel, flared open in front. Czech Republic. 8$\frac{1}{2}$" long, 4$\frac{5}{8}$" high.
(746) Crystal high heel with gold bow on front. Czech Republic. 7$\frac{3}{4}$" long, 4$\frac{1}{4}$" high.

(747) Blue shoe with applied green heel. Czech Republic. 6$\frac{5}{8}$" long, 3$\frac{1}{2}$" high.

(748) Teal high heel with a large flower ornament on the front. Lower half is solid glass. Czech Republic. 6" long, 6" high.

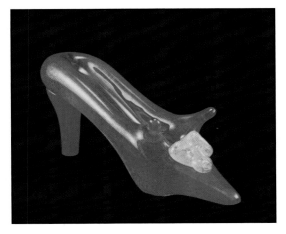

(750) Large cut glass Waterford shoe, promotion for "Slipper and the Rose." 9$\frac{1}{4}$" long, 5" high.
(749) Mottled orange shoe with opalescent ornament. Czech Republic. 6$\frac{1}{2}$" long, 2$\frac{3}{4}$" high.

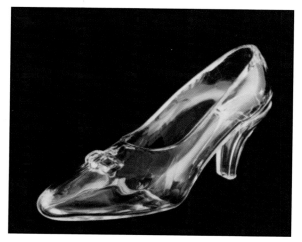

(751) Large crystal high heel with small buckle on the vamp. 8¼" long, 4½" high.

(752) Large crystal high heel with pointed toe. Austria. 7⅞" long, 5" high.

(753) Blue glass high heel with glue chip decoration. 8¾" long, 4¾" high.

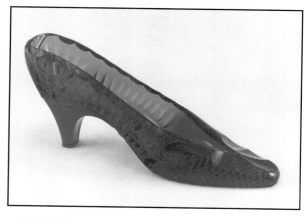

(754) Blue pressed glass pump with small Diamond pattern sole. 6½" long, 3" high.

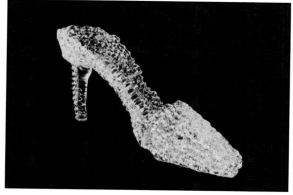

(755) Large spun glass shoe. 7¾" long, 3⅝" high.

(756) Large spun glass shoe with T-strap. 6⅞" long, 3½" high.

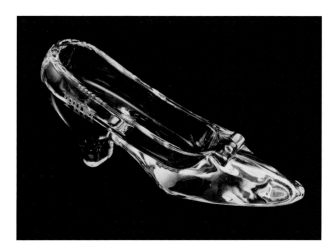

(757) Plain crystal pump with gold-painted bow. 5½ long, 2¾" high.

(758) Plain crystal pump, slightly shaped as a left shoe. No decoration or trim. 5¼" long, 3¾" high.

(759) Small crystal pump with high heel and Tiffin gold sticker. 3¼ long, 2⅜" high.

(760) Opaque blue shoe with frosted finish. Heel applied separately. 7½" long, 4¼" high.

(761) Blue shoe with coralene effect, outlined in gold. 7" long, 4⅜" high.

(762) Light amber shoe decorated with raised white enamel designs. 6³/₄" long, 4¹/₂" high.

This photograph shows the similarities and differences between (761) and (762). They are similar in size and shape but the decorations are entirely different. The blue one has a larger heel, a more pointed toe and larger top opening.

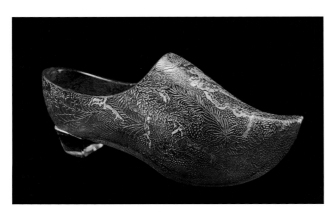

(763) Clog shape, crystal over cranberry with an applied crystal heel. 6³/₄" long, 3" high.

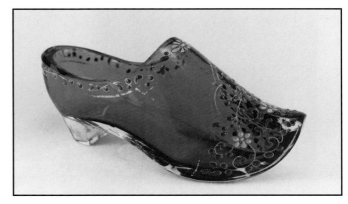

(764) Clog shape, crystal over cranberry. Same as (763) but different decoration, and smooth surface. 6³/₄" long, 3" high.

(765) Plain, clear glass shoe with a bow of garnets on the front. Rare, possibly one of a kind. 4" long, 1¹/₂" high.

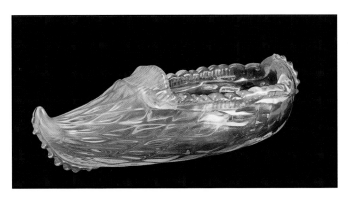

(766) Iridized, clog-shaped shoe that is mould blown. Diamond pattern, with pink rigaree from toe to sole. England. 7" long, 2¼" high.

(767) Plain, pump-style shoe with a small heel, slightly iridized. There is a coat of arms on the front. England. 8½" long, 3⅝" high.

(768) Beautiful amber slipper with a flat heel and small bow on the front. England. 9" long, 1¾" high.

(769) Large thin, blown crystal shoe with a small star or flower on the front. 9" long, 2⅞" high.

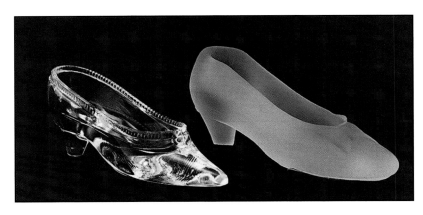

(770) Small crystal pump with vertical ribbing around the top edge. 4" long, 1⅞" high.

(771) Small frosted crystal pump with bow on the front. 4½" long, 2⅛" high.

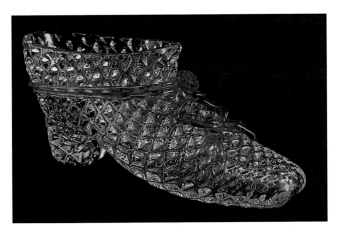

(772) Crystal shoe, mould blown with an all over Diamond pattern. Applied cranberry ribbon with raspberry on front. England. 6³⁄₄" long, 3¹⁄₈" high.

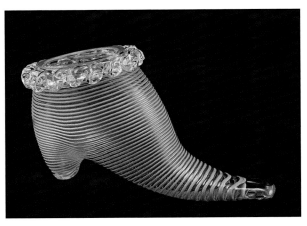

(773) Crystal slipper with blue threading and applied crystal rigaree around the top edge. England. 5" long, 2³⁄₄" high.

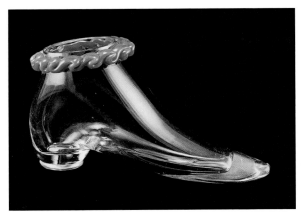

(774) Blown crystal shoe has opaque blue rigaree around the opening. England. 5¹⁄₄" long, 3" high.

(775) Opalescent vaseline blown shoe with applied vaseline rigaree around the edge. England. 3⁵⁄₈" long, 2³⁄₈" high.

(776) (777) Two blown crystal miniature shoes with applied crystal rigaree, unusual for shoes of this size. England. Both 2¹⁄₂" long. (776) is 1¹⁄₂" high; (777) is 1³⁄₄" high.

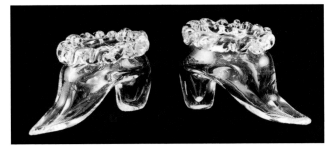

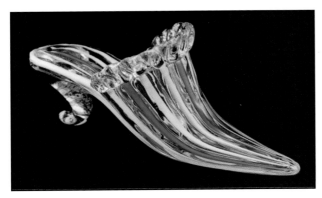

(778) Venetian shoe with alternating stripes of white and rose in crystal. 5" long, 2¹⁄₈" high

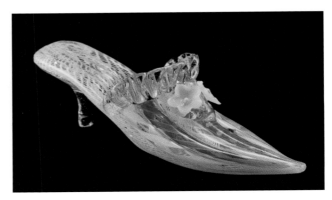

(779) The sole on this shoe is white latticino, and the front is twisted latticino in white, blue, pink and green. 5¹⁄₂" long, 2¹⁄₄" high.

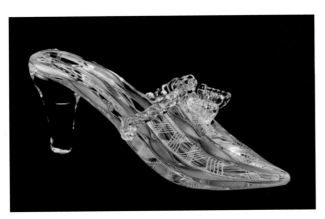

(780) Sole and front are made of rows of twisted white latticino and twisted green ribbon. Unusual crystal glass bow on the front. 5¹⁄₂" long, 2¹⁄₄" high.

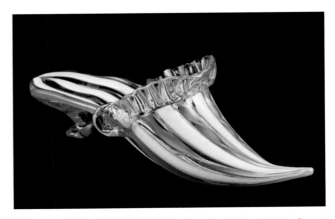

(781) This shoe has a sole of alternating stripes of amber and white. The top is stripes of white and twisted green. 6¹⁄₈" long, 2¹⁄₈" high.

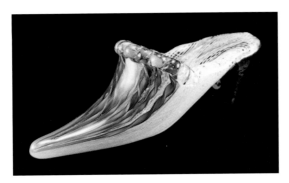

(782) Venetian shoe with white latticino sole and twisted green ribbons covering the top. 4⁵⁄₈" long, 1⁵⁄₈" high.

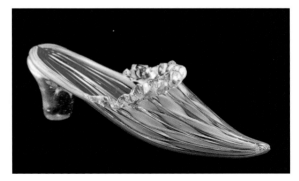

(783) Crystal, white and goldstone shoe with crystal ruffle. 5¼" long, 2" high.

(784) Crystal shoe with blue ribbons and a red sole. 4⅝" long, 1½" high.

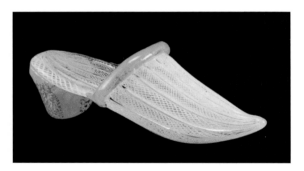

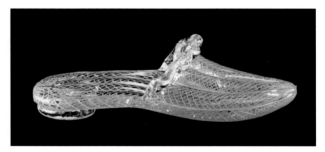

(785) All white latticino shoe with a yellow heel and rolled top edge. 4" long, 1½" high.

(786) All blue latticino shoe with a crystal ruffled top edge. This shoe has an unusually flat heel. 4¾" long, 1⅜" high.

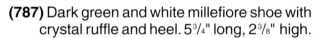

(787) Dark green and white millefiore shoe with crystal ruffle and heel. 5¾" long, 2⅜" high.

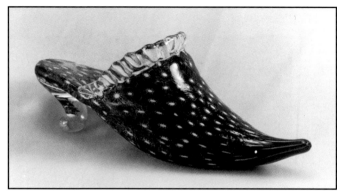

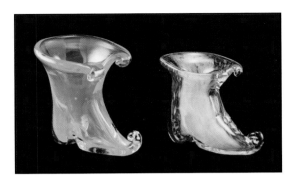

(788) Blue Diamond Quilted pattern, cased white on the inside. Frosted. 7¼" long, 2½" high.

(789) (790) Two small Italian glass boots with turned-up toes. Gold opalescent is 3¼" high and 3⅜" long; green opalescent is 2¾" high and 3¼" long.

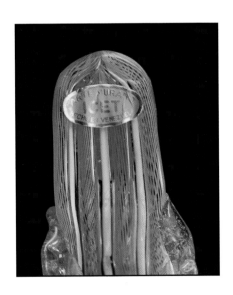

(791) Venetian glass boot with alternating stripes of white latticino and twisted ribbons in green, blue, pink and yellow. 3⅜" high, 3¾" long.

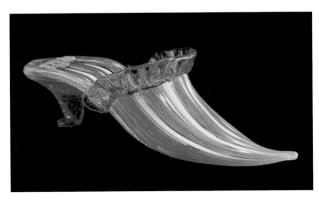

(792) This shoe was an interesting find, purchased at a flea market in 1996. In every way it resembles Italian shoes, but it has a label which reads ICET ARTE MURANO HECHO EN VENEZUELA. Apparently, this was a Murano-type shoe made in Venezuela. Shown above is the paper label on (792), revealing its Venezuelan origin. 6" long, 2" high.

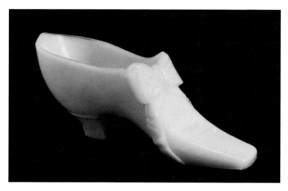

(793) Opaque white Gillinder shoe, sometimes called the Centennial shoe. 5¹/₂" long, 2¹/₂" high.

(794) Vaseline Gillinder shoe, same as (793) but a rare color. 5¹/₂" long, 2¹/₂" high.

(795) Gillinder shoe, same blue as (97) but covered with silver-colored metal webbing. Scarce. 5¹/₂" long, 2⁵/₈" high. (796) Amber Gillinder, same as (95) but covered with a metal webbing. 5¹/₂" long, 2⁵/₈" high.

(797) (798) (799) Gillinder high shoes. (797) is vertically ribbed like (134), but much more turquoise and trimmed in gold. 4¹/₄" high, 4¹/₄" long. (798) is the same as (141–142) (151), in vaseline. 4¹/₂" high, 4¹/₂" long. (799) is the same as (151), seated perfectly in a metal skate.

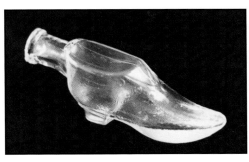

(826) Small cologne/perfume bottle with a neck opening at the back.Lightly stippled surface. 3½" long to end of neck, 1½" high.

(827) Cologne/perfume bottle shaped like a clog. there is a metal cap on the back opening. 3" long including cap, 1" high.

(828) Clog-shaped cologne/perfume with a back opening covered by a black cap. 3¼" long including cap, 1" high.

(830) Nailsea-type boot flask in cranberry with white looping. England. 7½" high, 3¾" wide, foot is 2⅜" long. **(831)** Nailsea-type boot flask in crystal with white looping. England. 8⅝" high, 3¾" wide, foot is 3" long.

(829) Nailsea-type boot flask in crystal with white looping. 9" high, 4" wide, foot is 3" long.

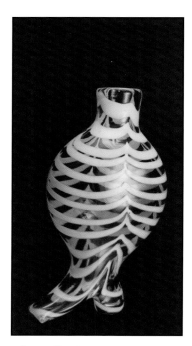

(832) Somewhat rounder Nailsea-type boot flask in crystal with wide looping. England. 6¹/₂" high, 3³/₈" wide, 2" long. **(833)** A short Nailsea-type boot flask with wide, white looping. England. 5" high, 2¹/₂" wide, 2¹/₈" long. **(834)** Boot flask in cranberry, yellow-green and opalescent spiral stripes. 7" high, 3¹/₂" wide, 2⁷/₈" long.

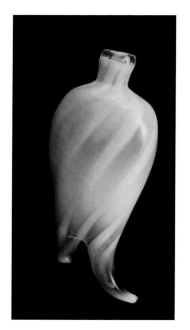

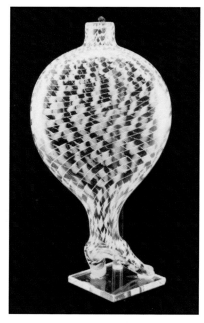

(835) Light green, spiral opalescent boot flask. England. 7³/₄" high, 3¹/₂" wide, foot 2³/₄" long.
(836) Crystal over blue boot flask. England. 5⁷/₈" high, 3³/₈" wide, foot 2¹/₂" long.
(837) Opalescent crystal boot flask with white spirals. 9" high, 4³/₄" wide, foot 2¹/₄" long.

(838) Spiral crystal boot flask, England. 6⅝" high, 3¾" wide, foot is 2" long. **(839)** Small plain crystal boot flask with original stopper. England. 5¾" high, 2⅞" wide, foot is 1½" long. **(840)** Crystal over amber boot flask. 6¾" high, 3¼" wide, foot is 2⅞" long.

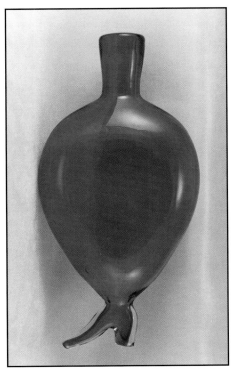

(841) Crystal over cranberry boot flask. 7⅝" high, 4" wide, 1¾" long.

(842) Flask similar to (841), 8½" high, 3¾" wide, foot 2⅝" long.

  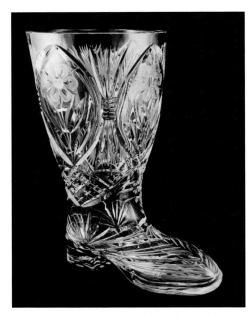

(843) Cut glass boot with spur. Paris. 5³/₄" high, 4³/₄" long. **(844)** Cut glass boot with applied heel. 7⁵/₈" high, 5" long. **(845)** Cut glass boot with applied heel. 7¹/₂" high, 5³/₈" long.

(846) Steuben cut glass boot with acid-etched mark on the heel (Fig. 65). 10³/₄" high, 6¹/₄" long.

(847) Crystal cut glass boot with a square toe and applied heel. 11" high, 7" long.

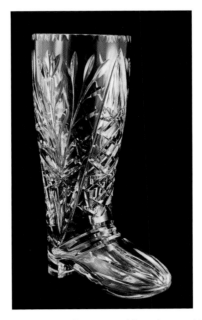

(848) Crystal cut glass boot with flowers on the front and back, and leaves on the sides. 9¹⁄₈" high, 6" long.
(849) Large cut glass boot with applied heel. 10⁷⁄₈" high, 6" long.
(850) Cut glass boot in green that has been cut back to crystal. 7³⁄₄" high, 5¹⁄₂" long.

(851) Small crystal boot, heavy for its size. 3³⁄₄" high, 3⁵⁄₈" long.

(853) (854) (855) Three small crystal boots, each having gold bands with etched grapes and grape leaves. Left boot is 5⁷⁄₈" high, 4" long; middle boot is 4¹⁄₄" high, 2⁷⁄₈" long; right boot is 3" high, 1⁷⁄₈" long.

(852) Small crystal boot, solid almost up to the frosted area. England. 2¹⁄₂" high, 2¹⁄₂" long.

(856) Stippled and smooth crystal boot, with a strap on the foot portion. 3" high, 1⁷⁄₈" long.

(857) (858) Two small crystal boots with straps and wrinkles at the ankle. It is not too difficult to see that the boot on the left is a copy of the one on the right, measuring 3¹⁄₈" high and 1³⁄₄" long. The original is 3³⁄₈" high and 1⁷⁄₈" long, with a hollow foot and polished top edge.

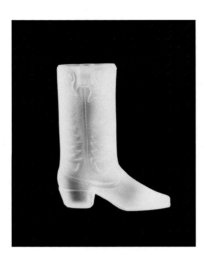

(859) Small, frosted cowboy boot. 3⁷⁄₈" high, 2⁷⁄₈" long.

(860) Crystal cowboy boot with RALPH LAUREN acid etched on the sole. Solid glass boot. 5" high, 3⁷⁄₈" long.

(861) Attached pair of opaque black boots. 2¹⁄₂" high.

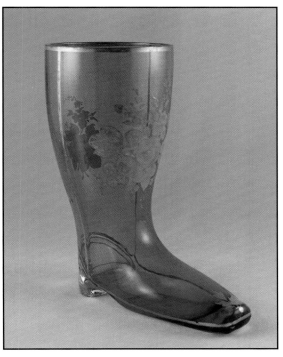

(863) Crystal over cranberry boot with enameled decorations. Top edge and heel trimmed with gold. 6⅝" high, 2⅞" long.

(862) Crystal over cranberry Bohemian boot with an applied heel. 7" high, 5¼" long.

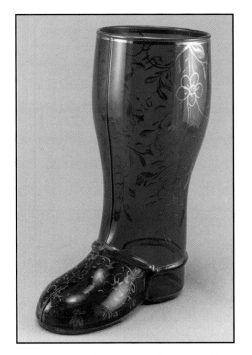

(864) Medium boot in cobalt blue, covered with painted flowers. 6⅝" high, 4⅛" long.
(865) Crystal over dark red. Decorated with silver and gold enamel. Germany. 6¼" high, 3⅛" long.
(866) Crystal Nailsea-type boot with white looping and a red rim. 8½" high, 2½" long.

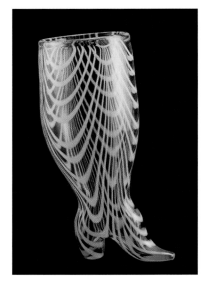

(867) Crystal Nailsea-type boot with white looping. 6¹/₈" high, 2¹/₂" long.
(868) Ruby-stained boot with strap and top edge in gold. Etched with FEDONA 1877. 6" high, 3⁷/₈" long.
(869) Medium crystal boot with applied heel and etched flowers on the front. 7¹/₂" high, 4⁵/₈" long.

(870) Yellow stippled boot, trimmed with gold. 6¹/₄" high, 3³/₄" long.

(871) Crystal boot with ruby-stained upper portion that is 2¹/₈" wide. 7³/₈" high, 4³/₈" long.

  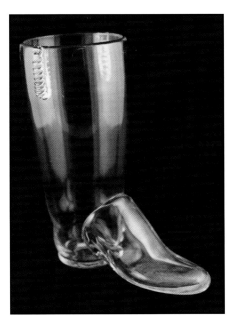

(872) This amber boot has been cut back to crystal. Front portion of the sole is in Diamond pattern. 5³/₄" high, 3¹/₈" long. **(873)** Frosted crystal over ruby boot with white enamel decorations. 6³/₄" high, 4" long. **(875)** Blown crystal boot with a rough pontil on the heel and rigaree straps on each side. 7¹/₂" long, 5³/₈" long.

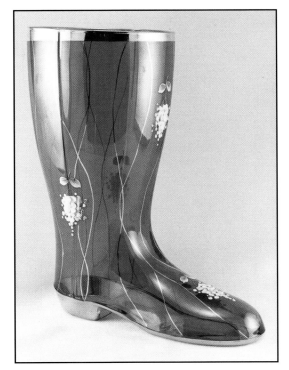 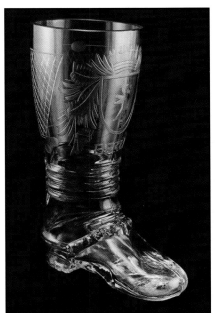 

(876) Medium boot, top half in amber cut to clear. Top half shows a bear within a shield. 6¹/₄" high, 3⁷/₈" long. **(877)** Like (876), amber boot with the top half cut to clear. Marked FRO-BELTURM OBERWEISSBACH THUR-WALD. 6¹/₄" high, foot is 3³/₄" long.

(874) Crystal over cranberry boot decorated with white enamel flowers. 9" high, 6³/₄" long.

(878) Crystal boot with metal strap and spur. The top of the boot is etched with a Diamond pattern. 9³⁄₈" high, 8¹⁄₂" long from toe to spur.

(882) (883) Medium boots, probably intended to be vases. The boot on the left is the same as (195) (197) with buttons on the right side. The boot on the right has buttons on the left side, indicating it came from a different mould. 7¹⁄₈" high, 4" diameter at the base.

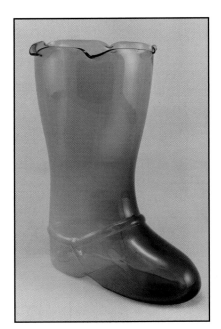

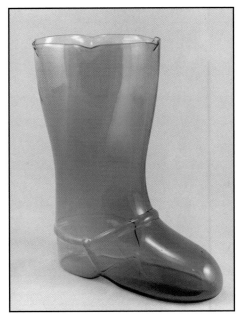

(879) Green boot of very thin glass, with a fluted edge. England. 5⁷⁄₈" high, 4³⁄₈" long.
(880) Amethyst boot with spirals, more pronounced on the inside. England. 5⁷⁄₈" high, 4³⁄₈" long.
(881) Turquoise boot, same as (879). England. 5⁷⁄₈" high, 4³⁄₈" long.

(884) Blown Nailsea-type stirrup in crystal with white looping. England. 3⁷⁄₈" high, 1³⁄₄" long.

(885) Blown Nailsea-type stirrup in crystal with white looping. England. 4¹⁄₂" high, 2³⁄₄" long.

(886) Blown crystal stirrup with etched leaves and marked A. BROWN 1884. England. 2⁷⁄₈" high, 2¹⁄₄" long.

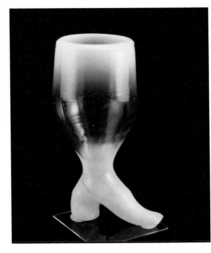

(887) Blown opalescent stirrup cup with applied green threading. 4" high, 2³⁄₈" long. **(888)** Blown opalescent vaseline stirrup. England. 4³⁄₈" high, 2" long. **(890)** Blown crystal over cranberry stirrup with vertical ribs. England. 3⁵⁄₈" high, 1¹⁄₂" long.

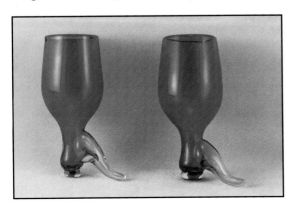

(889) Blown crystal over cranberry stirrup, 3³⁄₄" high.

(891) Blown cobalt stirrup cup with the pontil mark on the heel. England. 4" high, 2¹/₄" long.
(892) Swirled crystal stirrup with the pontil mark on the heel. England. 4³/₄" high, 2¹/₂" long.
(893) Blown crystal stirrup with attractive etching around the top. 4¹/₂" high, 2³/₈" long.

(894) Blown crystal stirrup with a cut Diamond pattern around the top. England. 3⁵/₈" high, 2³/₈" long.
(895) Blown crystal stirrup cup with frosted top and the initials R. S. England. 3⁷/₈" high, 2¹/₄" long.
(896) Blown crystal stirrup, with part of the top frosted and etched. England. 4" high, 2³/₈" long.

(897) Small, blown crystal stirrup cup with an applied foot in light green. England. 3" high, 1⁵⁄₈" long. **(898)** Unusual, blown crystal boot with the bottom half in solid glass. England. 3¹⁄₈" high, 1" long.

(901) Large, blown crystal stirrup with an applied foot. 5¹⁄₄" high, 3" long.

(899) Plain stirrup cup, measuring 3³⁄₈" high and 1³⁄₄" long. **(900)** Larger stirrup cup with an applied strip of glass that goes from the top edge to the heel. 4¹⁄₈" high, 1⁷⁄₈" long. Both purchased in England.

(902) Blown drinking boot with applied foot. The top two inches are frosted. 6¹⁄₂" high, 4¹⁄₂" long, 3¹⁄₂" diameter at the top. **(903)** Blown cobalt drinking boot with applied foot. 5⁵⁄₈" high, 3" long. **(904)** Blown, swirled drinking boot with applied foot. 7¹⁄₄" high, 3³⁄₄" long, 3⁵⁄₈" diameter at the top.

(905) Crystal boy in frosted crystal boot bottle. France, marked DEPOSE on the sole. Rare. 11½" high, 5" long.

(906) Large crystal Dutch shoe bottle with a raised leaf design on the front and sides. The shoe stands on the rear of the heel. 10⅝" high. (907) Same shoe as (906) but in frosted crystal.

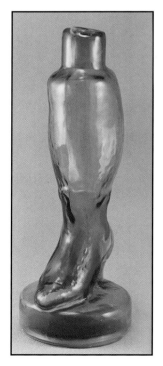

(910) Cobalt blue shoe bottle with ribbed foot portion. The top looks as if it originally had a cap or cover. England. 4⅜" high, 3¼" long.

(908) Carnival glass bottle of a leg and shoe on hassock. 7⅜" high, 2¾" diameter at base. (909) Blue glass bottle of leg and shoe on hassock. Same as (908).

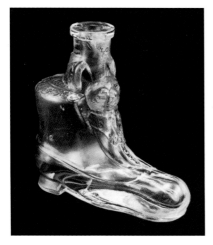  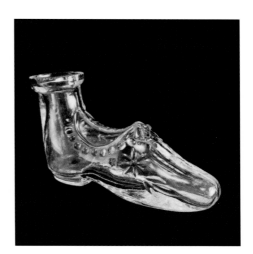

(911) Crystal cat in a shoe bottle with the remains of original COLOGNE label on its neck. 3⁷⁄₈" high, 3¹⁄₂" long. **(912)** Although it is difficult to make them out in the photograph, this shoe bottle is covered with the Old Woman in the Shoe and her children. 3³⁄₈" high, 3⁷⁄₈" long. **(913)** Crystal bottle in an unusual shape. It may have originally held cologne or perfume. 2⁷⁄₈" long, 1¹⁄₂" high.

(914) These photographs show a man's glass shoe decanter with the original stopper. The shoe has laces and stitching. Some of the ivory-colored glass has been painted tan and brown to resemble a real shoe. There is a metal collar with holders for six cordial glasses. Shoe is 7¹⁄₄" long, 5³⁄₈" high without the stopper. Photos courtesy of Anne Wojtkowski.

SPOON HOLDERS

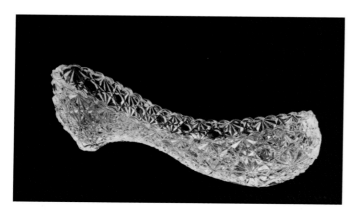

(915) Crystal Daisy & Button spoon holder. 7³/₈" long, 2³/₈" high.

(916) Blue Daisy & Button spoon holder. 7³/₈" long, 2³/₈" high.

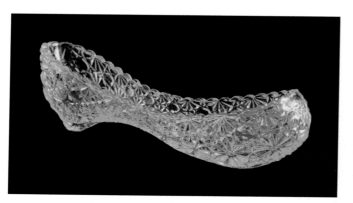

(917) Vaseline Daisy & Button spoon holder. 7³/₈" long, 2³/₈" high.

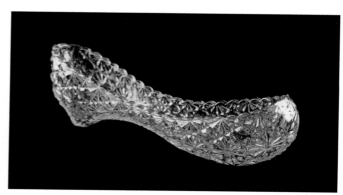

(918) This spoon holder is in light olive-green, not vaseline. It did not fluoresce when held under a black light. 7³/₈" long, 2³/₈" high.

(919) Cut glass spoon holder, different from the Daisy & Button pressed holders. Rare. 9¹/₂" long, 2¹/₄" high.

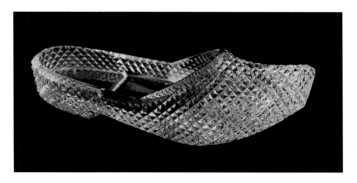

CONDIMENTS

(920) A lovely cut glass shoe, holding five pieces of a condiment set, each fitting in only one place. 7⅝" long, 5¼" high to top of cruet. Shoe itself is 1¾" high.

(921) Same Diamond pattern shoe as (920) but smaller. This one probably held a three-piece condiment set of salt, pepper and mustard jar. England. 6" long, 1½" high.

(923) Crystal shoe with a bow on the front. It holds salt and pepper shakers with silver-colored metal tops. Diamond pattern. 3¼" long, 3" high to top of shakers.

(922) Small, pressed glass cruet set with salt and pepper shakers, and mustard jar. 4⅞" long, 3¼" high to top of shaker, 1¾" high to top of shoe.

(924) Diamond pattern pressed glass shoe holding salt and pepper shakers with metal tops. 3¼" long, 3" high to top of shakers.

(925) Diamond pattern pressed glass shoe holding salt and pepper shakers with glass tops. 3" long, 2½" high to top of shakers.

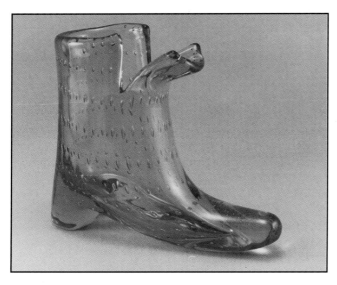

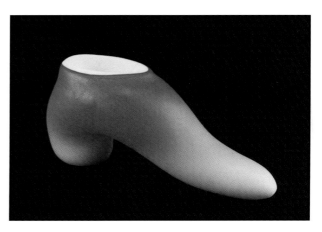

(926) Blown, blue glass short boot with controlled bubbles. Polished heel and sole. England. 6" long, 5³⁄₈" high.

(927) Small, blown cased shoe with a ground pontil mark on the heel. Creamy white inside; pink to dark red on the outside. England. 4" long, 2" high.

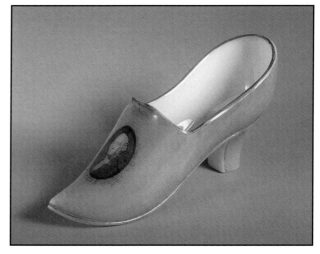

(928) Purple/white slag bootee with a mostly stippled surface. It has laces and five lace holes on each side. This shoe is scarce, 3³⁄₈" long, 2" high.

(929) Pink Libbey shoe with a transfer of George Washington on the front. Underneath is the date 1776. Possibly a Centennial souvenir. 6¹⁄₄" long, 3¹⁄₄" high. Photo courtesy of Anne Wojtkowski.

INDEX

A

advertising.....................97–99, 102–3, 106–8, 111, 117, 142, 160, *illustrated 48, 74, 135*

attached shoes..........................121, 146, 159, *illustrated 42, 80, 179, 188*

Atterbury & Company.............................7, 138

Austria (made in).............................135, 155, *illustrated 64–65, 135, 176*

aventurine...................130–1, 153, *illustrated 54*

B

B&H.......................118, 142, *illustrated 74, 118*

baby shoes...................................*see* bootees

Baccarat.............................134, *illustrated 62*

Baltimore Bargain House Catalog..............100, *illustrated 101*

Bamberger's Catalog..............155, *illustrated 155*

Basket Weave (pattern).............109, *illustrated 24*

Bean, George W. (patent).........118, *illustrated 118*

Belgium (made in).....................................114

Bellaire Goblet Company.....118, 140, *illustrated 36*

Bohemian...........................162, *illustrated 189*

boot jars.....................122, *illustrated 43, 45, 123*

bootees............7, 120, 142, 145, 152, 167, *illustrated 39–43, 74. 80–81, 94–95, 112, 152, 200*

bottle holders..........118, *illustrated 33–34, 36, 118*

bottles.................7, 114, 139, 142–6, 150, 160, 166, *illustrated 16, 19–20, 53, 69, 74–84, 88, 90–91, 139, 182, 196*

bouquet holders.......126–7, *illustrated 50–51, 127*

bow slippers.......................103, *illustrated 15, 19–20, 62–65, 103*

Boyd Crystal Art Glass...............9, 102–3, 111, 116–17, 145, *illustrated 15*

Bradley, Daniel R. (patent)...114–15, *illustrated 115*

Brauer, Firma R. O. & Co..........109, *illustrated 109*

Bryce Brothers...............100–103, 106, 138, 153, *illustrated 100–103*

Bryce, Higbee & Co....................................136

Burmese.............................132, *illustrated 59*

Burtles, Tate & Co.........128, 139, *illustrated 51–53*

Butler Brothers Catalog...............102–3, 107–8, 111, 122–3, 125–6, 136, 139, 142, 148, 153, *illustrated 102–3, 107–8, 111, 123, 125–6, 138–9*

C

Cambridge Glass Company.........................103

Cane (pattern).........................105–6, 109, 126, *illustrated 16–18, 23–24, 50–51*

carnival glass.........................125–7, 152, 166, *illustrated 49, 51, 94, 196*

Cat-in-Shoe.........................107, 140, 153, 166, *illustrated 19, 71, 96, 107, 197*

cat slippers......................102, *illustrated 13, 102*

Centennial Exhibition, 1876............108, 113, 138, 147, 158, 167, *illustrated 69, 158, 200*

Central Glass Company...............114, 116, 137, 153, *illustrated 66, 96, 115–16*

Challinor, Taylor & Company.......................111, *illustrated 28, 112*

chevron............................112, *illustrated 27, 112*

Chinese shoes.................106, *illustrated 18, 106*

cocktail shaker..................148, *illustrated 84–85*

cologne, perfume and scent bottles.........99–100, 114, 118–19, 139, 142, 144–50, 160, *illustrated 10, 12, 16, 32, 34, 36, 69, 74, 78, 80–84, 91, 138–9, 147, 182–3, 197*

Columbia Glass Company.......102, *illustrated 102*

Columbian Exposition......*see* World's Columbian Exposition

condiment sets......140, 167, *illustrated 70–71, 199*

Coral (pattern)...................102, *illustrated 13–14*

Coralene...........................156, *illustrated 171–2*

cranberry.....................127, 130–32, 141, 149, 156–7, 159–60, 162–4, *illustrated 50, 54, 57, 59, 172, 180–1, 183–5, 189, 191, 193*

Crescent Glass Company.....124, *illustrated 46–47*

Crockery & Glass Journal............................138

"Crystal Slipper"...................97, 99, *illustrated 97*

Cube (pattern)........136, 146, *illustrated 66–67, 80*

Czechoslovakia (made in)....................145, 151, *illustrated 80, 93*

Czech Republic (made in).........155, *illustrated 169*

D

Daisy & Button (pattern)............97–100, 102–6, 111, 113–14, 119, 121, 134, 137–9, 142, 144, 146, 153, 167, *illustrated 10–18, 27–29, 37, 39, 42–43, 62, 66–68, 80, 95–96, 101–4, 115, 138*

Daisy & Square (pattern).........109, 114–15, 144, 146, *illustrated 23–24, 32, 78, 80, 114, 144*

Davidson and Company............149, *illustrated 88*

decanters........................150, 166, *illustrated 89*

Degenhart Crystal Art Glass Company.........9, 102–3, 111, 116, 121, 145, *illustrated 15, 102–3*

Denmark (made in)...............134, 147, *illustrated 83–84, 147, 196*

Diamond (pattern)....................99, 104, 116, 120, 134–5, 137, 140, 144–5, 153, 155–7, 167, *illustrated 10–11, 15, 33–35, 41, 62–66, 78, 80, 96, 104, 170, 173–4, 192, 194, 199*

Diamond Block (pattern)............116, *illustrated 33*

Diamond Quilted (pattern)..................151, 157, *illustrated 93, 177*

Duncan, George & Sons..................97, 99, 100, 105, 111, 121, 152, *illustrated 10–11, 27–28, 42–43, 78, 80, 98–99, 105, 144, 152*

Dutch shoe (clog)...................129, 134, 140, 153, 156, 159–60, 166, *illustrated 52–53, 62–63, 71, 96, 172–3, 179, 183, 196*

E

England (made in)..................110, 114, 127–31, 134, 139–41, 145, 153, 156–7, 159–61, 163–7, *illustrated 25, 31, 56, 62, 71–72, 78, 88, 173–4, 182, 184–5, 192, 194–6, 200*

English Pressed Glass..............................149

F

fasteners................100–101, 125, *illustrated 101*

Fenton Art Glass Company............9, 94, 111, 121, 126, 152, *illustrated 94–95, 152*

Finecut (pattern)............100, 105, 115, 118, 122, 140, 152, *illustrated 12, 16, 31–32, 36, 152*

Finland (made in)...............147, *illustrated 83–84*

Fishscale (pattern)..............102, *illustrated 13–14*

flasks...............141, 160, *illustrated 72–73, 183–5*

France (made in).........114, 116, 143–4, 149–50, 166, *illustrated 35, 62, 78, 80, 90–91, 134*

G

Germany (made in).........119, 140, 159–60, 162, *illustrated 37–38, 69, 71, 181–2, 189*

Gillinder & Sons............107–8, 111, 113, 138–9, 158–9, 166, *illustrated 21–22, 28–29, 69, 108, 111, 158, 178*

H

Hazel Atlas Company...............................142

Heisey Glass Company.............134, *illustrated 62*

Hobbs, Brockunier & Co.......138, *illustrated 67–68*

Hurlbut, James (design)..........118, *illustrated 118*

I

Illustrated Historical Register of the Centennial Exposition (1876)................................158

Imperial Glass Company...........143, *illustrated 77*

inkwells...................7, 122, 139, *illustrated 45, 69, 77,122–3*

Inwald, Josef..............135, *illustrated 64–65, 135*

Ireland..............................159, *illustrated 181*

Italy...........................132–3, 149–50, 157, *illustrated 59–61, 86, 90–91, 175–7*

K

Kanawha Glass Company........103, *illustrated 103*

Kastrup Glassworks...........147, *illustrated 83, 147*

kat slipper...................................*see* cat slipper

King Glass Company..............104, 120–1, 136, *illustrated 39, 42, 66–67, 104*

kitten slipper.............................*see* cat slipper

L

Ladies' Home Journal.................99, *illustrated 97*

lamps............................138, *illustrated 69–70*

Lancaster Glass Company.........................125

last.................97, 100, 102–5, *illustrated 98, 105*

latticino.................133, 157, *illustrated 61, 175–7*

Lee, Ruth Webb.........7, 113, 128–9, 136, 158, 161

Legras & Cie..............149–50, *illustrated 88, 149*

Leonard's, H. & Sons...............112, *illustrated 112*

Leslie, Frank....................................158

Libbey Glass Company............107, 128–9, 167, *illustrated 52–53, 129, 200*

Lornita Glass.........................121, *illustrated 42*

M

man's shoe.........107, 122, 124, 140, 142, 159–60, *illustrated 19, 43, 45–47, 71, 74, 107, 124, 181–2*

match holders......101, 116, 122, 136–7, 140, 159, *illustrated 33, 35, 45, 66–67, 70–71, 104, 115, 122, 136–7*

millefiore..........132–3, 157, *illustrated 59–61, 176*

Miller, John E. (patent)...........97–98, 100–1, 121, *illustrated 98*

milk glass.............................*see* opaque white

Mosser Glass, Inc............110, 112, *illustrated 110*

Murano.......................................*see* Venetian

N

Nailsea...........................141, 160, 162, 164, *illustrated 72–73, 183–4, 189–90, 193*

National Export Exposition, 1899.................107

New England Glass Company...................129, *illustrated 53*

New Martinsville Glass Company.................101

New York World's Fair, 1939.......120, *illustrated 40*

O

Old Virginia Glass.....................................152

opaque white glass............100, 102–3, 106–110, 113, 116, 118, 120–31, 135–6, 138–40, 142–6, 152–3, 158–9, *illustrated 12, 17, 25, 29, 31, 33, 35–36, 42–44, 46, 48–52, 54–58, 64, 69–71, 74, 76–77, 80–82, 95–96, 178–9, 107, 111, 140*

P

Pilgrim Glass Company......151, *illustrated 92, 151*

pitchers..144, 146

Pottery, Glass & Brass Salesman...............125, *illustrated 125*

Q

QVC Network......................155, *illustrated 170*

R

roller skates..........................105, 113–17, 153, *illustrated 31–33, 35, 96, 115–16*

rubina.............130, 132, 149, *illustrated 54, 59, 88*

rubina verde..........................131, *illustrated 56*

ruby..............124, 144–5, 148–9, 152, 161, 163, *illustrated 46, 85–86, 78–79, 191*

ruby-stained...........97, 99, 111, 126, 143, 162–3, *illustrated 10–11, 28, 76–77, 48–49, 190*

S

salts and shakers...........140, 144, 146–7, 167, *illustrated 74, 83*

sandals.........................106, 140, 147–8, 167, *illustrated 18, 106*

shoe lamp......................138, *illustrated 69–70*

slag.................108, 111–12, 120, 135, 144, 146, 149, 152, 167, *illustrated 21–22, 25, 27–28, 40, 65, 78, 80, 87–88, 112, 179, 200*

Smith, Henry J. (patent).................100, 102–3, *illustrated 100–1*

Smith, L. E. Glass Company......114, *illustrated 114*

Sollers, S. D. & Co..........97, 99, 117, *illustrated 98*

Sowerby & Company............108, 110, 135, 140, *illustrated 21–22, 25–26, 64–65, 71, 108*

Sowerby peacock mark.........108, 110, 135, 140, 153, *illustrated 25–26, 64–65, 108, 117*

Spangled...................................*see* Spatter

Spatter.............130–1, 153, *illustrated 54–58, 96*

Spelman Brothers Catalog..................124, 147, *illustrated 106, 124, 147*

Spinning Wheel, The........150, *illustrated 163, 165*

spoon holder......................167, *illustrated 198*

spun glass...............146, 155, *illustrated 80, 170*

St. Louis Fair of 1904...............................150

Steuben...........................161, *illustrated 161*

stirrup cups.......................127, 141, 164–5, *illustrated 50, 72–73, 164–5, 193–5*

Sweden (made in).......109, 134, *illustrated 62, 109*

T

Tappan, Herman...............105, 116–17, 126, *illustrated 34, 50–51, 127*

thimble holders............................144–6, 159, *illustrated 78–80, 82*

Thimble Society of London.........................146

threaded.....................................142–3, 160

thumbprint.................111–12, *illustrated 27, 112*

Tutbury, Ltd...140

U

U. S. Glass Company.................................99

V

Vasart...153

vaseline..............97, 99–109, 111, 113–14, 117–18, 120–22, 124, 126–7, 135, 137–8, 144, 152–3, 157–8, 164, 167, *illustrated 10, 12–16, 18–20, 22–23, 28, 34–36, 41–42, 46–47, 50, 65–66, 78, 94, 104, 174, 178, 193, 198*

Venetian.......132–3, 157, *illustrated 59–61, 175–7*

Venezuela..........................157, *illustrated 177*

Venice...132–3

Victorian...............110, 141, *illustrated 20, 27, 73*

Victorian Glass.......113, 128–9, 136, 148, 158, 161

W

Wales Goodyear & Company.......................142

Wallace, R. P. & Company.........112, 120–21, 126, *illustrated 40, 42, 50, 112*

Washington, George (president)..................167, *illustrated 200*

Waterford crystal......................120, 155, 159, *illustrated 41, 169, 181*

West Virginia Specialty Glass.....148, *illustrated 85*

World's Columbian Exposition, 1893......107, 146, *illustrated 20*

Wright, L. G. Glass Company.................106, 152

BIBLIOGRAPHY

Baltimore Bargain House Catalog, March 1903.

Barret, Richard Carter. *Identification of American Art Glass*. Manchester, Vermont: Forward's Color Productions, 1964.

Bickenheuser, Fred. *Tiffin Glassmasters, Book III*. Grove City, Ohio: Glassmasters Publications, 1985.

Bredehoft, Neila M. and Tom. *Victorian Novelties and Figurals, George Duncan & Sons*. St. Louisville, Ohio: Cherry Hill Publications, 1989.

Bredehoft, Neila M., George A. Fogg and Francis C. Maloney. *Early Duncan Glassware*. 1987.

Brothers, J. Stanley (Patent Files). Rakow Library, Corning Museum of Glass.

Butler Brothers Catalogs, 1888–1918.

Covill, William E., Jr. *Ink Bottles and Inkwells*. Taunton, Massachusetts: William S. Sullwold, 1971.

Davis, Derek C. and Keith Middlemas. *Colored Glass*. New York: Clarkson N. Potter, Inc., 1968.

Ferson, Regis F. and Mary F. *Yesterday's Milk Glass Today*. Pittsburgh: self-published, 1981.

Fitzpatrick, Paul J. "Gillinder & Sons at the Philadelphia Centennial." *The Spinning Wheel*. July-August 1965, 14–15.

Florence, Gene. *Degenhart Glass and Paperweights*. Cambridge, Ohio: Degenhart Paperweight and Glass Museum, 1982.

Frank Leslie's Illustrated Historical Register of the Centennial Exposition, 1877. 216–17, 267.

Gillinder & Sons Catalog, c. 1880.

Godden, Geoffrey. *Antique Glass and China*. New York: Castle Books, 1966. (Published by arrangement with A. S. Barnes & Co., Inc.)

Gores, Stan. "Gillinder's 'Fancy Goods' Prices Then and Now." *The Spinning Wheel*. May-June 1980, 34–35.

Heacock, William. *Rare and Unlisted Toothpick Holders*. Marietta, Ohio: Antique Publications, 1984.

_____. *The Glass Collector, No. 4*. Marietta, Ohio: Antique Publications, 1982.

Heacock, William and Fred Bickenheuser. *Encyclopedia of Victorian Colored Pattern Glass, Book 5, U. S. Glass From A to Z*. Marietta, Ohio: Antique Publications, 1978.

Holmes, Edwin F. *Thimbles*. 1976.

_____. *A History of Thimbles*. 1985.

Husfloen, Kyle. *Collector's Guide to American Pressed Glass, 1825–1915*. Radnor, Pennsylvania: Wallace-Homestead Book Company, 1992.

James, Margaret. *Black Glass*.

Ladies' Home Journal, Christmas 1890. Curtis Publishing Company, Philadelphia.

Lattimore, Colin R. *English 19th Century Press-Moulded Glass*. London, England: Barrie & Jenkins, Ltd., 1979.

Lee, Ruth Webb. *Victorian Glass*. Wellesley Hills, Massachusetts: Lee Publications, 1944. (13th Edition)

Long, Jennie D. *An Album of Candy Containers*. Kingsburg, California: T. O. Long and J. D. Long, 1978. (Second Printing)

_____. *An Album of Candy Containers, Volume 2*. Kingsburg, California: T. O. Long and J. D. Long, 1983.

Lucas, Robert Irwin. *Tarentum Pattern Glass*. Tarentum, Pennsylvania: Robert I. Lucas, 1981.

Manley, Cyril. *Decorative Victorian Glass*. New York: Van Nostrand Reinhold, 1981.

McDonald, Anne Gilbert. *Evolution of the Night Lamp*. Des Moines, Iowa: Wallace-Homestead Book Company, 1979.

Measell, James and Don E. Smith. *Findlay Glass*. Marietta, Ohio: Antique Publications, 1986.

Measell, James and W. C. "Red" Roetteis. *The L. G. Wright Glass Company*. Marietta, Ohio: Antique Publications, 1997.

Miller, Everett R. and Addie R. *The New Martinsville Glass Story*. Marietta, Ohio: Richardson Publishing Co., 1972.

Murray, Sheilagh. *The Peacock and the Lions*.

Newman, Harold. *An Illustrated Dictionary of Glass*. London, England: Thames and Hudson, Ltd., 1977.

Post, Robert C., Ed. *1876, A Centennial Exhibition*. Washington, DC: Smithsonian Institute, 1976.

Pullin, Anne Geffken. *Glass Signatures, Trademarks and Trade Names*. Radnor, Pennsylvania: Wallace-Homestead Book Company, 1986.

Revi, Albert Christian. *American Pressed Glass and Figure Bottles*. Camden, New Jersey: Thomas Nelson, Inc., 1964.

Spillman, Jane Shadel. "American and European Pressed Glass in the Corning Museum." *The Corning Museum of Glass Catalog Series*. 1981.

_____. "A Collector's Choice. Some 19th Century Glasses from the Strauss Collection." *The Spinning Wheel*. March-April 1981, 36.

Slack, Raymond. *English Pressed Glass 1830–1900*. London, England. Barrie & Jenkins, 1987.

Spinning Wheel, The. "Whimsical Figure Bottles in Glass." March 1963, 24.

Spelman Brothers Catalog, Spring 1886.

Shoes of Glass, 2

1998 VALUE GUIDE

BY LIBBY YALOM

Like everyone who has written a price guide, I dislike doing so. When determining the price for a shoe, there are too many variables that factor in such as location of the purchase; whether the shoe was bought at an antique show, antique shop or flea market; whether the purchaser is a dealer buying for resale or a collector buying for a personal collection; and so on.

The following prices are based on availability and mint condition. In as much as this value guide is intended to be only a *guide*, the author, contributing collectors, dealers and the publisher cannot warranty any of the listed prices. The value of shoes is constantly changing and all prices may certainly fluctuate from those listed depending upon the cirucmstances of the sale.

In a few instances, I have indicated RARE as the value. In those cases, the shoes are the only examples I have ever seen in over 25 years of collecting, so it is impossible to establish a value. Should collectors come across any of these RARE shoes, they will have to decide for themselves what they are willing to pay.

Finally, neither the publisher nor the author can accept responsibility or liability for losses incurred by persons using this guide as the basis for any transaction, whether due to typographical errors or other reasons.

Figure	Price	Figure	Price	Figure	Price	Figure	Price
Plate 1		27A	$ 50.00	*Plate 6*		95	$ 155.00
1	$ 55.00	28	45.00	64	$ 45.00	96	80.00
	w/advertising	29	45.00	64A	40.00	97	125.00
1A	175.00	30	45.00	65	45.00	98	110.00
2	55.00	31	48.00	66	140.00	98A	110.00
3	55.00	32	150.00	67	165.00	99	145.00
4	90.00	33	50.00	68	45.00	99A	145.00
	w/advertising	34	45.00	69	150.00	99B	170.00
	and bottle	35	48.00	70	65.00	100	170.00
5	60.00	36	45.00	71	55.00		
6	75.00			72	55.00	*Plate 9*	
6A	75.00	*Plate 4*		73	45.00	101	48.00
7	55.00	37	48.00	74	45.00	102	28.00
	w/advertising	37A	55.00	75	45.00	103	28.00
7A	60.00	38	65.00	75A	40.00	103A	28.00
8	125.00	39	45.00	76	65.00	104	75.00
9	75.00	40	45.00	76A	40.00	104A	90.00
	w/bottle	41	45.00	76B	40.00	105	48.00
10	50.00	42	45.00			106	50.00
10A	50.00	43	45.00	*Plate 7*		107	48.00
11	130.00	44	50.00	77	110.00	107A	50.00
12	50.00	45	45.00	78	125.00	108	50.00
		46	75.00	78A	130.00	109	105.00
Plate 2		47	75.00	79	110.00	109A	105.00
13	55.00	48	75.00	80	55.00	109B	105.00
14	80.00			81	60.00	110	105.00
	w/bottle	*Plate 5*		82	55.00	111	50.00
15	55.00	49	56.00	82A	75.00	112	90.00
16	60.00	50	52.00	83	55.00	113	100.00
17	60.00	51	52.00	83A	75.00	114	90.00
18	60.00	52	35.00	84	175.00		
19	60.00	53	50.00	84A	175.00	*Plate 10*	
20	50.00	54	48.00	85	62.00	115	60.00
20A	55.00	55	48.00	86	100.00	115A	60.00
20B	50.00	56	48.00	87	65.00	115B	60.00
21	45.00	57	48.00	88	145.00	115C	60.00
22	45.00	58	55.00	88A	145.00	116	49.00
23	45.00	59	35.00			117	75.00
24	45.00	60	60.00	*Plate 8*		117A	85.00
		60A	60.00	89	47.00	118	110.00
Plate 3		60B	60.00	89A	70.00	118A	60.00
25	70.00	61	85.00	90	47.00	118B	60.00
	w/advertising		w/bottle	91	85.00	118C	65.00
26	140.00	62	190.00	92	75.00	119	50.00
26A	160.00	62A	190.00	93	80.00	119A	50.00
26B	170.00	63	190.00	94	80.00	119B	55.00
27	45.00						

Figure	Price	Figure	Price	Figure	Price	Figure	Price
120	$ 110.00	150A	$ 85.00	*Plate 15*		211	$ 60.00
121	75.00	151	85.00	183	$ 65.00	212	60.00
122	60.00	152	85.00	184	65.00	213	65.00
123	50.00			183–84	140.00 pr	214	60.00
124	125.00	*Plate 13*		185	68.00		
125	75.00	153	85.00	186	68.00	*Plate 18*	
126	75.00	154	65.00	185–86	145.00 pr	215	50.00
		155	175.00	187	65.00	216	50.00
Plate 11		156	85.00	187	105.00 w/bottle	217	50.00
127	65.00	157	85.00			218	50.00
127A	68.00	158	85.00	188	65.00	219	50.00
128	85.00	159	85.00	187–88	140.00 pr	220	80.00
129	85.00	160	125.00 w/bottle	189	55.00	221	50.00
130	65.00	161	75.00	190	65.00	222	50.00
131	150.00	161A	75.00	191	65.00	223	50.00
132	65.00	161B	75.00	190–91	140.00 pr	224	55.00
133	65.00	162	100.00	192	75.00	225	50.00
134	110.00	163	65.00	192A	75.00	226	50.00
135	90.00	164	65.00	193	75.00		
136	60.00	165	65.00	194	75.00	*Plate 19*	
136A	70.00	166	65.00			227	40.00
137	75.00			*Plate 16*		228	38.00
138	60.00	*Plate 14*		195	145.00	229	35.00
		167	70.00	196	175.00	230	35.00
Plate 12		168	65.00	196A	175.00	231	40.00
139	60.00	169	40.00	196B	175.00	232	55.00
139A	60.00	169A	40.00	197	145.00	233	55.00
140	60.00	170	46.00	198	70.00	233A	55.00
139–140	130.00 pr	170A	46.00	198A	70.00	234	RARE
140A	60.00	170B	46.00	198B	70.00	235	125.00
141	75.00	170C	46.00	199	160.00	235A	125.00
142	75.00	171	48.00	200	120.00	236	65.00
143	65.00	172	75.00	201	75.00	237	60.00
143A	65.00	172A	75.00	202	85.00	238	60.00
143–143A	140.00 pr	173	65.00	202A	150.00	239	60.00
144	125.00	174	75.00			240	75.00
145	125.00	175	75.00	*Plate 17*		240A	90.00
146	125.00	176	75.00	203	30.00	241	75.00
147	60.00	177	65.00	204	50.00	242	75.00
147A	60.00	177A	75.00	204A	60.00		
147B	60.00	178	65.00	205	25.00	*Plate 20*	
147–147B	130.00 pr	179	40.00	206	25.00	243	120.00
148	60.00	180	46.00	207	55.00	243A	50.00
148A	60.00	181	75.00	207A	60.00	244	120.00
149	60.00	182	65.00	208	45.00	245	120.00
148–49	130.00 pr			209	60.00	246	120.00
150	85.00			210	35.00	247	120.00

Figure	Price	Figure	Price	Figure	Price	Figure	Price
248	$ 65.00	276	$ 30.00	*Plate 24*		334	$ 110.00
248A	65.00	276A	85.00	307	$ 110.00	334A	120.00
248B	65.00	277	30.00	307A	110.00	334B	120.00
249	65.00	277A	75.00	307B	125.00	334C	120.00
250	65.00	277B	55.00	308	65.00	335	120.00
251	60.00	278	35.00	308A	75.00	336	120.00
252	60.00	279	35.00	309	65.00	337	120.00
253	60.00	279A	35.00	310	130.00	338	110.00
254	60.00	279B	35.00	310A	150.00	339	150.00
255	95.00	280	40.00	311	165.00	339A	150.00
255A	105.00	281	40.00	311A	165.00	339B	110.00
255B	95.00	282	35.00	311B	165.00	339C	140.00
255C	95.00	283	35.00	311C	130.00	340	120.00
255D	105.00	284	35.00	312	65.00	340A	120.00
255E	115.00	285	35.00	313	65.00	340B	120.00
255F	115.00	285A	35.00	313A	70.00	340C	120.00
256	95.00	286	35.00	314	165.00	341	150.00
257	95.00	286A	35.00	315	165.00	342	110.00
257A	105.00	286B	40.00	316	150.00	343	110.00
		286C	40.00	317	150.00		
Plate 21		287	35.00	318	110.00	*Plate 27*	
258	95.00	288	40.00	319	90.00	344	90.00
259	95.00			319A	90.00	344A	90.00
260	95.00	*Plate 23*				344B	90.00
261	95.00	289	80.00	*Plate 25*		344C	90.00
262	105.00	289A	100.00	320	150.00	345	80.00
263	105.00	290	75.00	320A	175.00	345A	80.00
264	95.00	291	75.00	321	130.00	346	80.00
264A	100.00	292	75.00	322	120.00	347	95.00
264B	120.00	293	75.00	323	120.00	348	90.00
264C	100.00	294	35.00	324	120.00	349	95.00
265	95.00	294A	125.00	324A	120.00	349A	95.00
266	25.00	295	35.00	324B	110.00	350	75.00
267	25.00	296	35.00	325	120.00	351	80.00
267A	35.00	297	35.00	326	145.00	352	80.00
268	25.00	298	35.00	327	110.00	353	75.00
269	25.00	299	160.00	327A	110.00	354	80.00
269A	35.00	300	150.00	328	145.00	355	80.00
270	25.00	301	150.00	329	110.00	356	150.00
271	25.00	302	125.00	330	145.00	357	150.00
272	25.00	303	125.00	331	120.00	358	90.00
273	25.00	304	75.00			359	98.00
		305	75.00	*Plate 26*			
Plate 22		306	150.00	332	110.00	*Plate 28*	
274	30.00			332A	120.00	360	110.00
275	30.00			333	150.00	361	110.00

Figure	Price	Figure	Price	Figure	Price	Figure	Price
362	$ 110.00	394A	$ 185.00	425	$ 185.00	464	$ 20.00
363	110.00	395	45.00	426	150.00	465	20.00
364	110.00	396	40.00	427	40.00	464–65	45.00 pr
365	100.00	397	45.00	428	45.00	466	140.00
366	100.00	398	160.00	429	135.00	467	65.00
367	100.00	398A	160.00	430	45.00	468	55.00
368	100.00	398B	160.00	431	45.00	469	65.00
369	100.00	399	40.00	432	45.00	470	48.00
370	125.00	400	40.00				
371	100.00	401	45.00	*Plate 35*		*Plate 38*	
372	100.00	402	45.00	433	375.00	471	55.00
373	100.00	403	150.00	434	275.00	471A	55.00
374	110.00	404	150.00	435	375.00	472	50.00
375	100.00	405	150.00	436	150.00	472A	50.00
376	85.00	406	150.00	437	175.00	473	60.00
377	85.00	407	150.00	438	150.00	473A	60.00
				439	150.00	473B	60.00
Plate 29		*Plate 32*		440	185.00	473C	60.00
378	160.00	408	150.00	441	150.00	474	55.00
379	150.00	408A	150.00	442	150.00	474A	90.00
380	75.00	409	150.00			474B	100.00
381	45.00	410	150.00	*Plate 36*		475	75.00
382	115.00	411	150.00	443	350.00	475A	75.00
382A	140.00	412	175.00	444	200.00	476	65.00
382B	175.00	412A	175.00	445	225.00	476A	65.00
383	RARE			446	125.00	477	90.00
384	90.00	*Plate 33*		447	150.00	477A	90.00
385	50.00	413	950.00	448	150.00	478	48.00
385A	60.00	413A	1,100.00	449	150.00	479	33.00
		413B	1,050.00	450	85.00	480	28.00
Plate 30		414	1,000.00	451	175.00	481	45.00
386	170.00	415	195.00	452	200.00	482	25.00
387	185.00	416	RARE	453	200.00	483	48.00
388	130.00	417	250.00			484	38.00
388A	180.00	418	100.00	*Plate 37*		484A	38.00
388B	150.00	418A	110.00	454	48.00	485	38.00
388C	185.00	419	300.00	455	120.00	486	25.00
389	170.00	420	65.00	456	45.00	487	25.00
389A	180.00			457	45.00	488	25.00
390	170.00	*Plate 34*		458	75.00	489	20.00
391	170.00	421	250.00	458A	85.00	490	20.00
392	180.00	421A	300.00	459	45.00	491	30.00
393	170.00	422	650.00	460	50.00	492	21.00
		423	40.00	461	37.00	493	21.00
Plate 31		424	150.00	462	37.00	494	35.00
394	175.00	424A	120.00	463	44.00		

Figure	Price	Figure	Price	Figure	Price	Figure	Price
Plate 39		527	$ 130.00	559A	$ 40.00	581A	$ 300.00
495	$ 95.00	528	125.00	560	35.00	581B	175.00
495A	95.00	528A	125.00	561	37.00	582	55.00
496	95.00	528B	125.00	561A	40.00	583	46.00
497	95.00	528C	125.00	562	28.00	584	150.00
498	185.00	529	125.00	563	24.00		
499	125.00	530	125.00	563A	24.00	*Plate 47*	
499A	125.00	531	75.00	564	35.00	585	30.00
499B	125.00	532	75.00			586	30.00
499C	125.00	533	125.00	*Plate 42*		587	30.00
500	25.00	533A	130.00	565	450.00	588	30.00
501	25.00	533B	150.00		w/glasses	589	30.00
502	25.00	534	45.00	565A	650.00	590	30.00
503	25.00	535	75.00		w/glasses		
504	25.00	536	32.00	565B	550.00	*Plate 48*	
505	25.00	537	25.00		w/glasses	591	155.00
506	110.00	538	60.00			591A	155.00
507	110.00	538A	75.00	*Plate 43*		592	45.00
508	26.00	539	25.00	566	130.00	593	28.00
509	32.00	540	50.00	566A	130.00	594	28.00
510	32.00	541	16.00	567	200.00		
511	32.00	542	140.00	568	130.00	**(Plates 49 – 54 have**	
512	32.00	542A	150.00	569	65.00	**deliberately been omitted.)**	
513	32.00	543	16.00	569A	65.00		
514	155.00	544	15.00	569B	30.00	*Plate 55*	
514A	165.00	545	65.00	570	65.00	712	40.00
515	140.00	546	65.00			713	40.00
515A	150.00	547	150.00	*Plate 44*		714	22.00
516	140.00	547A	150.00	571	75.00	715	25.00
516A	140.00	547B	140.00	572	200.00	716	28.00
516B	140.00	548	25.00	573	80.00	717	38.00
517	140.00	549	25.00	574	175.00	718	25.00
517A	150.00			574A	175.00	719	40.00
518	140.00	*Plate 41*		574B	175.00	720	40.00
518A	140.00	550	32.00	574C	RARE	721	22.00
519	150.00	551	18.00	575	RARE	722	38.00
520	140.00	551A	18.00			723	40.00
521	150.00	551B	18.00	*Plate 45*		724	40.00
		552	45.00	576	80.00	725	30.00
Plate 40		553	45.00	577	50.00	726	35.00
522	45.00	554	48.00	578	70.00	727	45.00
523	60.00	555	50.00	579	85.00	728	40.00
524	45.00	556	50.00			728A	40.00
525	45.00	557	40.00	*Plate 46*		728B	40.00
526	40.00	558	30.00	580	50.00	728C	40.00
526A	50.00	559	32.00	580A	50.00	728D	35.00
				581	250.00	728E	40.00

Figure	Price	Figure	Price	Figure	Price	Figure	Price
728F	$ 45.00	*Iridized*		*High Button*		833	$ 225.00
728G	45.00	766	$ 175.00	800	$ RARE	834	400.00
		767	160.00	801	125.00	835	225.00
Plate 56				802	130.00	836	200.00
729	135.00	*Pumps*				837	250.00
730	85.00	768	175.00	*Clogs*		838	200.00
731	80.00	769	75.00	803	75.00	839	150.00
732	50.00	770	20.00	804	50.00	840	140.00
733	150.00	771	10.00	805	125.00	841	300.00
734	155.00					842	300.00
735	120.00	*Rigaree and Ribbon*		*Miniatures*			
736	75.00	772	RARE	806	40.00	*Boots*	
737	95.00	773	175.00	807	22.00	843	375.00
738	105.00	774	140.00	808	22.00	844	125.00
739	70.00	775	180.00	809	55.00	845	175.00
740	85.00	776	62.50	810	85.00	846	325.00
741	65.00	777	62.50	811	85.00	847	150.00
742	70.00			812	160.00	848	100.00
743	78.00	*Venetian*				849	175.00
744	48.00	778	95.00	*Men's Shoes*		850	130.00
		779	110.00	813	175.00	851	75.00
High Heels		780	120.00	814	140.00	852	105.00
745	300.00	781	120.00	815	65.00	853	25.00
746	250.00	782	95.00	816	70.00	854	20.00
747	85.00	783	90.00	817	45.00	855	15.00
748	300.00	784	80.00			856	125.00
749	200.00	785	75.00	*Scents/Colognes*		857	20.00
750	1,200.00	786	95.00	818	250.00	858	75.00
751	150.00	787	100.00	819	200.00	859	40.00
752	100.00	788	75.00	820	125.00	860	40.00
753	RARE	789	45.00	821	175.00	861	125.00
754	60.00	790	45.00		leg on card	862	300.00
755	45.00	791	125.00	822	95.00	863	190.00
756	45.00	792	85.00		leg only	864	50.00
757	30.00			823	75.00	865	90.00
758	50.00	*Gillinder*		824	22.00	866	300.00
759	45.00	793	150.00	825	22.00	867	300.00
		794	RARE	826	40.00	868	110.00
Decorated		795	160.00	827	35.00	869	120.00
760	150.00	796	160.00	828	20.00	870	80.00
761	900.00	797	120.00			871	75.00
762	300.00	798	125.00	*Flasks*		872	200.00
763	300.00	799	RARE	829	350.00	873	65.00
764	300.00		w/skate	830	375.00	874	225.00
765	RARE			831	350.00	875	160.00
				832	225.00	876	80.00

Figure	Price	Figure	Price	Figure	Price	Figure	Price
877	$ 75.00	892	$ 175.00	*Bottles*		918	$ 140.00
878	75.00	893	175.00	905	$ RARE	919	RARE
879	50.00	894	175.00	906	250.00		
880	50.00	895	175.00	907	250.00	*Condiment Sets*	
881	50.00	896	175.00	908	20.00	920	225.00
882	145.00	897	160.00	909	20.00	921	85.00
883	145.00	898	160.00	910	90.00	922	45.00
		899	150.00	911	110.00	923	30.00
Stirrups		900	160.00	912	175.00	924	30.00
884	175.00	901	170.00	913	50.00	925	30.00
885	175.00			914	RARE		
886	175.00	*Drinking Boots*				*Miscellaneous*	
887	250.00	902	350.00			926	100.00
888	250.00	903	200.00	*Spoon Holders*		927	150.00
889	175.00 ea	904	450.00	915	140.00	928	95.00
890	200.00			916	160.00	929	165.00
891	185.00			917	140.00		

NOTES

NOTES